ENGLISH PAPER PIECING • 16 QUILT PROJECTS

hexa
go-go

Tacha Bruecher

stashBOOKS
an imprint of C&T Publishing

Text copyright © 2012 by Natasha Bruecher

Photography and Artwork copyright © 2012 by C&T Publishing, Inc.

Publisher: Amy Marson

Creative Director: Gailen Runge

Editor: Cynthia Bix

Technical Editors: Sandy Peterson and
Sadhana Iyengar Wray

Cover/Book Designer: Kristy Zacharias

Page Layout Artist: Kerry Graham

Production Coordinator: Jessica Jenkins

Production Editor: S. Michele Fry

Illustrator: Tim Manibusan

Photography by Christina Carty-Francis
and Diane Pedersen of C&T Publishing,
Inc., unless otherwise noted

Published by Stash Books, an imprint of C&T Publishing, Inc., P.O. Box 1456,
Lafayette, CA 94549

Library of Congress Cataloging-in-Publication Data

Bruecher, Natasha, 1976-

  Hexa-Go-Go : English paper piecing : 16 quilt projects / Natasha Bruecher.

    p. cm.

  ISBN 978-1-60705-357-6 (soft cover)

  1. Quilting--Patterns. 2. Patchwork--Patterns. 3. Hexagons. I. Title.

  TT835.B755 2012

  746.46--dc23

                    2011034026

Printed in China

10 9 8 7 6 5 4 3 2 1

contents

Dedication

For Amelie, Hanna, and Luis: Ihr seid die Besten in der ganzen Welt!

Acknowledgments

Thank you to Cynthia, Diane, and Susanne for your help throughout the writing of this book. You are all brilliant.

Thank you to Nina from http://1001quilt.de for your help in quilting the *Over the Rainbow* and *Dropped Diamonds* quilts.

A huge thank-you to Luis for keeping me going and for keeping the girls amused while I worked! You mean everything to me.

Thank you, Mum and Dad, for your encouragement in everything I take on.

A huge thank-you to everyone I have met through Flickr and who helped me take my quilting to a new level—in particular the members of Bee Inspired.

Lastly, I want to thank my *Fat Quarterly* family—Katy, Brioni, John, Kate, Nova, and Aneela. You guys rock!

Foreword

Being in general a fairly impatient type, I never thought I would take to English paper piecing. Too much work, too much time. But in reality I find it highly therapeutic. Snuggled up on the couch in the evening, at the playground with my girls, or on a long car ride, I take my hexagons with me. One or two here and there, and before you know it you have a block. They are the perfect fit for an urban quilter. Hexagons can be slipped into your bag and stitched up in no time on the commuter train. They are so wonderfully portable—quilting's answer to knitting!

Most quilters I come across are a bit apprehensive about hexagons. I find that they would like to try a project but are not sure where to start or how to make a quilt that is contemporary looking. Cast away your fears with this book. Learn how forgiving hexagons are and how you don't need to make an entire Grandmother's Flower Garden quilt to be a hexagon quilter.

The projects in this book combine some of the current quilting trends with hexagons, but none are 100 percent hexagons. Each project takes traditional hexagons and adds a modern twist such as wonky piecing, white sashing, embroidery, or raw-edge appliqué.

Many of the projects are perfect for using up scraps. Whether you are drowning in a fabric stash that you wouldn't use up even if you sewed from now to eternity, or you just have a few odds and ends tucked away at the back of the cupboard, you will find a project in here for you.

I also have included some time-saving concepts from the quilting world. The *Over the Rainbow* quilt (page 107) is the result of an online quilting bee called Bee Inspired, for which I sent fabric to 18 other quilters worldwide so they could each make one of my hexagon blocks. They sent the finished blocks back to me, and the result is this fabulous quilt. *Modern Grandmother's Flower Garden* (page 114) is quilted using the quilt-as-you-go method and shows that you can quilt a queen-size quilt on your home machine.

Hexagons are so wonderfully portable—quilting's answer to knitting!

introduction

what is english paper piecing?
and do i have to be english to do it?

Hmm…good question! I think it is only coincidence that I am English. I certainly got my first taste of English paper piecing in needlework classes at my school in England. But having lived in the United States and now in Germany, I am pretty confident in saying that you can be any nationality!

English paper piecing is a technique in which fabric is basted to paper templates and then hand stitched together to form tessellations. The technique dates back to eighteenth-century England. The first hexagon pattern was printed in 1835 in the American magazine *Godey's Lady's Book*. At this time all things English were highly fashionable in America, and hence it was called English paper piecing for marketing purposes. Nowadays it would be called something terribly high tech and complicated such as "digitally generated template technique," or perhaps "iPatch"!

English paper piecing can be used for shapes such as diamonds, triangles, hexagons, pentagons, and so forth. This book concentrates on the hexagon because it is one of the most versatile shapes. The wide angles in a hexagon make basting easy, and the hexagon shape can be used by itself to make lots of patterns without introducing other shapes.

This book contains projects for everyone. Small, quick projects are offered for those with a busy lifestyle or who are new to English paper piecing. For readers who are experienced with hand stitching and quiltmaking, more involved patterns are included.

hand stitched?

Yes, I did say hand stitched! And you might well ask, "Why—in this day and age of sewing machines—do I want to learn this technique?" There are a number of reasons.

English paper piecing (EPP) allows for much better piece alignment than machine piecing. It is easy to get all your points and corners to match up. You can tackle complicated projects with the confidence that your finished project will look great.

EPP is portable. While I was working full time, I rarely got to my sewing machine. With EPP, I can take my sewing project with me wherever I go. The commute to work became my sewing time. Now at home with my small children, I can slip some hexagons into my bag—or into my *Go Faster Box Bag* (page 132)—and stitch to my heart's content while my children play in the park.

Hand stitching is amazingly therapeutic. It gives you time to sit still and think—something we forget to do these days. Your hands are busy, and yet your mind can wander. My main problem is that while I am stitching, I am busy thinking up more projects that I want to stitch!

making your projects modern

Modern and *contemporary* are labels open to all sorts of interpretation. But in general, design factors such as color palette, fabric choice, and block settings are all important in giving your project a modern edge.

Color palette

Plenty of places will spark inspiration for modern color palettes. My favorite place to go is the photo-sharing site Flickr.com. Check out all sorts of images—not just those showing quilts—to find different color palettes that inspire you. Such photos also can help you visualize how different proportions of color can create different effects in your quilts.

Images courtesy of Brooke Biette (apriltwoeighty.com)

Hexagon quilts are great for making a feature of your favorite prints. If you already have a great modern print you want to use, then pick out colors from within that print to make your color palette. This is even easier if the selvage has color dots printed on it.

When planning your color palette, remember how important different values are in creating lively, interesting quilts. Value is the lightness or darkness of a color; all quilts need some contrast in values to make them pop. Are most of the colors you have chosen light to medium value? Then choose a darker value to complement them, and vice versa.

Fabric choice

I like to use many different prints of each color in my color palette to make my quilts more interesting. Rather than using
a yard of one print, I would rather use fat quarters of four or
five different prints of the same color. I find that this adds
depth and keeps the viewer's eye moving around the quilt.

Try breaking away from the usual quilting fabric choices; there is
no need to stick to quilting cotton. Combine them with fabrics
like linen or voile to give your quilts added texture and depth.

Consider stamping or stenciling your own designs on solids to
fussy cut. Why not stamp some letters, washing symbols, or
other simple motifs? All you need are some simple supplies.
Use a purchased rubber stamp or carve a design onto an eraser.
Grab an ink pad or acrylic fabric paint such as Liquitex Soft
Body Acrylic Colors (available from C&T Publishing), and follow
the manufacturer's directions to stamp and set your design.

You can also stencil designs using freezer paper and fabric paint. For
stenciling instructions, see the *Stars and Stripes* quilt (page 141).

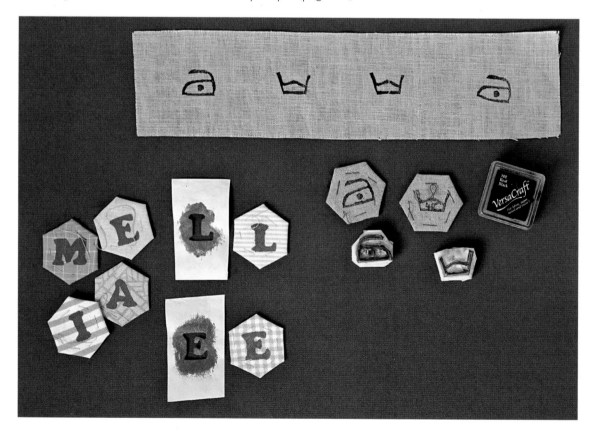

Block settings

Hexagons are nothing new; they have been used in quilts for centuries. However, traditional hexagon quilts tend to be made using hexagons alone, without borders or other block settings. To make your quilt designs stand apart from traditional hexagon quilts, try mixing hexagons with different blocks and borders.

Hexagon rosettes are combined with string blocks in the *Cat Tails* quilt (page 46).

The best way to give the hexagons in your designs a more modern feel is to think of the hexagon as a design element in the same way you might think of a half-square triangle. Like half-square triangles, hexagons can be used singly or sewn together to create other shapes such as rosettes, stars, and diamonds. These shapes can then be used as design elements to frame blocks—as borders or as central motifs.

The *Stars and Stripes* quilt (page 138) features strips of hexagons.

Another way to use hexagons is to stitch some hexagons together and treat the finished piece as you would any other piece of fabric. Just cut it up into strips or blocks, and sew these into your project.

The *Sunday Brunch Place Mat* (page 104) has a block of hexagons sewn into its center.

Just as you wouldn't restrict yourself to only one size of half-square triangles in a quilt, you needn't limit your projects to only one hexagon size. Mix small and large hexagons in your design.

Detail from the *Giant Star Pillow* (page 82) shows more than one size of hexagon in a single, small project.

Design Note

If you want to play with creating your own hexagon-based designs, grab some hexagonal graph paper and sketch to your heart's content! This paper comes in various hex sizes (see Resources, page 159).

Remember, too, that hexagons can be used in projects of all sizes, from a needle book to a bag or from a pillow to a quilt. You can appliqué single hexagons to almost any sewn project. No project is too big or too small for a sprinkling of hexagons!

The projects in this book are grouped in sections to show how different hexagon design elements can be used in your sewing projects. You will find projects using rosettes, diamonds, stars, blocks of hexagons, and free-form hexagons. I hope they inspire you to experiment with hexagons in your own quilt designs.

quilt with friends

If some of the larger quilt projects in this book seem a little daunting, why not enlist the help of your friends? One of my favorite things is working with a group of friends to create a quilt. Quilting bees, whether virtual or run by your local guild, are a great way to meet other quilters, learn new techniques, and just have fun!

A quilting bee is a group of quilters who work together to make blocks for one another's quilts. The ones I have taken part in have been structured so that each month, a different member asks the other members of the bee to make a certain type of block. The following month it's another member's turn, and so on, until all members have had blocks made for them. I have been involved in many bees on Flickr. The easiest way to find a bee that is looking for participants is to log on to flickr.com/groups/quiltingbeeblocks/.

Why not break some of the larger quilt projects in this book into smaller sections and ask each of your bee members to make a section for you? The *Over the Rainbow* quilt (page 107) was created with the help of Bee Inspired members.

getting started
with hexagons

Before making your quilt or other chosen project, you will create the hexagon components. In this chapter, you'll find an overview of the tools, supplies, and techniques you will use. Also, this chapter has advice on quilting and binding your quilt.

what do i need?

You will need relatively few supplies to get started. Essentially, these include paper hexagon templates, over which you'll hand stitch your cut fabric hexagons. Beyond that, you'll want some quilter's tools and supplies as described in this chapter. Most of these are probably things you already have.

Hexagon templates

The most important tool is the paper template. You can buy die-cut paper templates. Or you can make your own using the template patterns in the back of this book (pages 157 and 158) or use patterns downloaded from the Internet. For online template sources, see Resources (page 159).

Die-cut templates are great because they are exact, and you can save a lot of time that you would otherwise spend printing and cutting your own templates. However, they do come with a price tag.

PAPER

If you want to make your own templates, you can use any type and weight of paper. The heavier the paper, the better it will maintain its shape during basting. You will get crisper edges on the corners of your fabric hexagons if you use paper that is slightly heavier than ordinary printing paper. However, lighter-weight paper is easier to fold and tuck out of the way when you are sewing together hexagons, and it is much lighter when you are working on large sections. Try a number of different types until you find the one you like best. Here are examples of paper that I have used:

- Index cards
- Cardstock (slightly lighter weight than index cards)
- Old greeting cards
- Printing paper
- Leftover uncolored pages from kids' coloring books
- Freezer paper

tip Warning: Don't use magazines or papers with a lot of print or color on them. The inks or colors could transfer onto your fabric. I once used a colored-in page from my kids' coloring book. Oops! I won't do that again.

Freezer paper is great because it eliminates the need for pins. Use your iron to adhere the freezer-paper template to the fabric, and off you go. But be careful when basting the hexagon corners; it is easy to fold the freezer paper out of shape. If you want to use freezer paper for your templates, try Quilter's Freezer Paper Sheets from C&T Publishing. You can feed these sheets into your printer to print multiple templates.

Whichever paper you choose for a project, be sure to use only that type of paper for the *whole* project. Slight differences in the weight of the paper could affect the size of your hexagons.

See Making Templates (page 18) to learn how to make paper templates.

Pins and gluestick

Use pins to hold fabric hexagons in place while basting them to the paper templates (see Making Hexagons, page 20). I use dressmaker pins with as small a head as possible. I find that my thread often gets caught and tangled on pins with larger heads, which is very irritating!

Make sure you have a pincushion at hand for your needles and pins, especially if you are anything like me. After the simplest thing, even a telephone call, I forget where I put my needle. I spend the next 30 minutes telling the children to back away and frantically looking for the misplaced needle! Better yet, make the *Rosette Needle Book* (page 32) to keep yourself safe and organized!

As an alternative to pins, use a dab of water-soluble glue from a gluestick. The glue keeps the paper template in place for as long as needed, but the paper can be removed easily when you have finished sewing. All traces of the glue are removed when you wash your quilt.

Scissors and rotary cutters

You need two pairs of scissors. Paper blunts scissors, so make sure you use one pair for cutting paper templates and the other pair for cutting fabric. If you are like me, it might be a good idea to label which is which!

You also need a rotary cutter and a quilter's cutting mat.

Needles and thread

Needles also can be blunted by paper. Use an old needle for basting and a quilting needle for sewing the hexagons together. You will need either betweens or milliner's/straw needles, size 10, 11, or 12, depending on your personal preference.

Choose a bright thread for basting. Dig out threads that you never use and ones that contrast with your fabric to make removal easier.

When stitching the hexagons together, choose a thread that best matches the color of your fabric. When stitching dark and light fabrics together, the stitching is less likely to show if you use a thread that matches the darker fabric. If in doubt, choose gray! Sometimes prints can have an array of colors, and it is difficult to choose which thread might suit best. Gray blends in surprisingly well with most colors.

To sew your hexagons together, use a strong polyester thread or a thread that is designed specifically for hand stitching. Pulling thread repeatedly through the fabric causes significant friction, and some threads will fray and break easily. This can be very frustrating.

> **tip** Running your thread through beeswax or Thread Heaven Thread Conditioner and Protectant (available at quilt and fabric shops) can help prevent tangles in your thread when hand stitching.

Thimble

Repeatedly drawing the thread through the hexagons will eventually make your fingers sore where the thread rubs against them. To prevent this, use a metal or flexible thimble or a simple adhesive bandage. You can also use plastic protectors. I love using these self-adhesive pads that stick to your fingertips. Thimble-It and a variety of other brands designed for sewing are available in quilt and fabric stores. They are thin enough that you forget they are there, and they stick really well. They even stayed put after I washed the dishes!

If your hands start aching too much, then it's time to take a break! Switch for a while to an element of your project that is not hand-sewn, or cut fabric for your next project.

Plastic zippered bags and rubber bands

How I love these bags! They are fantastic for protecting paper templates, basted hexagons, and parts of your project. Stack the basted hexagons, secure them with rubber bands, and then pop them into a zippered bag.

techniques

Following are techniques for making the hexagons and for sewing them to each other or appliquéing them to a background. Also included are general suggestions for quilting and binding your quilts.

Making templates

Hexagons are measured by the length of their sides; for example, 1″ hexagons are those with each side measuring 1″. The template patterns in this book are the following sizes: ½″, ¾″, 1″, 1½″, 1¾″, and 2″ (page 157).

These template patterns do not include seam allowances. The size of the template pattern is the size of the finished hexagon. When you cut the fabrics, you have to add ¼″ seam allowances.

Note that the largest distance across the hexagon is always twice the length of each side. This is helpful in planning your designs.

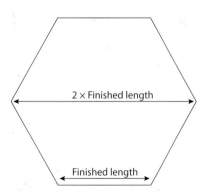

You need a template for each fabric hexagon you want to make. Copy and print the number of hexagons called for in your project. Accurate templates are critical for English paper piecing, so cut out your templates as carefully as possible.

tip You can make the job go more quickly if you cut out multiple templates at once. Staple multiple paper sheets together to prevent the layers from shifting and then cut out the templates.

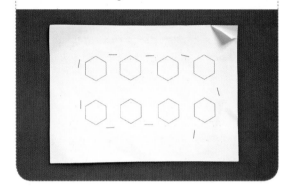

Most paper templates are reusable, so look after them well. Pop them into a zippered bag labeled with the size of the hexagon.

If you want to fussy cut hexagons from print fabric, create transparent plastic templates. Draw around your paper template on a piece of template plastic, add a ¼″ seam allowance on all sides, and cut out. Place the plastic template on the right side of the fabric and position it over the motif you want to use. Draw around the plastic template, and cut out the fabric hexagon.

Use plastic templates to fussy cut.

tip To make removing paper templates easier, try punching a hole using a paper punch in the center of each paper template before you use it. The hole makes it easier for you to get a grip on the paper when removing it.

Cutting fabric hexagons

Make sure your fabric is freshly pressed. It is difficult to remove slight wrinkles or creases later, and they could distort your work.

Although it is good practice to ensure that the grain of the fabric always runs in the same direction, the joy of English paper piecing is that the paper holds the shape of the fabric, so you can get away without cutting on the grain.

If you are not fussy cutting, you can cut your fabric into strips, and then cut those strips into squares as indicated in each of the projects. Place a paper template on top of each square, on the *wrong* side of the fabric, and trim the fabric to a hexagon shape, leaving ¼″ all around for seam allowances.

Some people like to leave the square untrimmed and fold and baste the edges of the fabric square over the paper template. I *don't* do this because it creates unnecessary extra fabric in the seams and can make quilting a bumpy experience. But use whatever method works best for you.

> **tip** To save time, use a rotary cutter to trim a stack of five or six squares at once, depending on the thickness of the fabric.

Rotary cut a stack of hexagons.

Pin each template to a cut fabric hexagon through the center using a single pin. Alternatively, use a dab of glue from a gluestick.

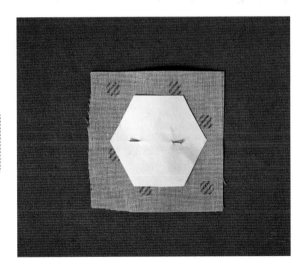

Making hexagons

Now it's time to baste the fabric hexagons to the templates.
The two most widely used methods are presented in this section.

Figure 1

Figure 2

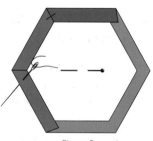

Figure 3

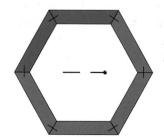

Figure 4

BASTING METHOD 1

With this method, you baste through both the seam allowance and the paper template.

1. Thread a needle with bright, contrasting thread. Fold the seam allowance over the template along one side. Leave about a 3″-long thread tail and bring your needle through all the layers (fabric, paper, and seam allowance) from the bottom to the top (Figure 1).

2. Fold over the next side and stitch over the corner, bringing your thread back through the seam allowance, paper, and fabric, to secure in place (Figure 2).

3. Continue around all the sides of the hexagon (Figures 3 and 4).

4. Leave a 3″-long tail and cut the thread. *Do not knot your thread, so it will be easier to remove later.*

This method is great for making sure the fabric is held tight against the paper template—particularly important when making larger hexagons. *For larger hexagons, you might want to sew more than once through the paper template on each side of the hexagon to make sure the fabric is held in place properly.*

> **tip** If you use pins to hold the paper template on the fabric, remove them as soon as you have basted your fabric; if left in for a long time, they can leave permanent holes.

Figure 5

Figure 6

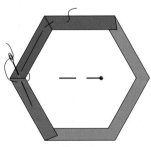

Figure 7

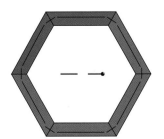

Figure 8

BASTING METHOD 2

With this method, you baste through only the seam allowance, not through the paper template.

1. Thread a needle with bright, contrasting thread and fold the seam allowance over the template along one side. Leave a 3″-long tail and take your needle down through the seam allowance from the top to the bottom (Figure 5).

2. Fold over the next side. Bring the needle back through to the top of the seam allowance on the other side of the corner. Backstitch over the corner without stitching through the paper template (Figure 6). For information on the backstitch, see Hand Stitches (page 23).

3. Fold over the next side and take your needle back down through the seam allowance from the top to the bottom, just before the corner. Bring the needle back through to the top on the other side of the corner. As before, backstitch over the corner (Figure 7).

4. Repeat for all the sides and corners. The basting can be secured by sewing the first corner again (Figure 8). *Do not knot your thread.*

The benefit of this method is that you don't need to remove your basting stitches, because they won't show, which is a great time-saver. The paper templates can be easily popped out of the hexagons when you are finished, and the remaining basting stitches help the hexagon keep its shape for appliqué. I would recommend using this method only for hexagons *smaller* than 1¾″. With paper templates 1¾″ or larger, if you baste through only the seam allowance, you may find that the fabric does not lie flat against the paper template. This will cause you headaches when stitching the hexagons together.

Sewing the hexagons together

Now your hexagons are ready to use in the projects of your choice. You can appliqué them singly to a background fabric (see Appliquéd Hexagons, page 24), or you can sew them into more complex shapes either to appliqué or to use in piecing. To sew hexagons together, use one of several stitches as shown in Hand Stitches (page 23).

Figure 9

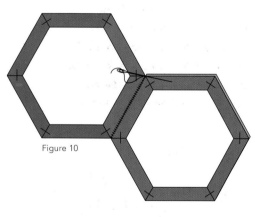

Figure 10

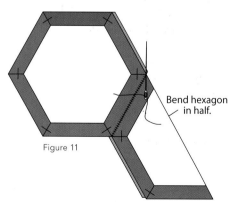

Bend hexagon in half.

Figure 11

> **tip**
>
> The number of hexagons in some of the larger projects in this book can seem a little overwhelming at first. But don't worry! All the projects can be broken down into smaller units that can be sewn together at the end. Invest in some zippered bags to keep the different units organized!

1. To sew hexagons together, cut off a manageable length of strong thread. It is tempting to use as long a thread as possible, but longer threads can get tangled, and you will spend more time sorting out knots than sewing! About 18″ is a good length. Run your thread through Thread Heaven Thread Conditioner and Protectant or beeswax to help it glide smoothly through the fabric and to prevent breakage.

2. Place 2 hexagons right sides together. Secure the thread by stitching 3 or 4 times in the same place (Figure 9). Stitch along the edges, using the stitch of your choice.

3. Open up the hexagons and add a third hexagon. Put the hexagons you want to sew together with right sides facing. Start sewing at the inside corner (Figure 10). To strengthen the corner where the hexagons meet, take a couple of stitches in the same place. Stitch along the edges using the stitch of your choice.

4. Make a few stitches in the same place at the end of the seam and knot to secure. Cut the thread.

5. To stitch the remaining seam, open up the 3 hexagons. Place the 2 hexagons to be sewn together, right sides facing. Bend the third hexagon in half to do this (Figure 11). Start at the inside corner, take a few stitches in one place to secure, and then work your way along the edge using the stitch of your choice.

6. At the end of the joined seam, make a few stitches in the same place to secure, and cut the thread.

hand stitches

You can choose various stitches to sew your hexagons together. In addition to the three stitches shown, you can also use a running stitch, but be sure to use small stitches close together. I prefer the whipstitch, but experiment to find which suits you best.

Whipstitch

This is the most common stitch used to join hexagons together (Figure 12).

Place 2 hexagons right sides together. Insert your needle from the back, and sew only through the fabric right at the fabric folds (not through the paper) on the back and front hexagons. Pull the stitch tight, and bring your needle through from the back to the front again.

Take as shallow a stitch as possible—about 1/16″ apart—so that you don't go through the paper as well as the fabric and so that your stitches will be invisible on the right side.

Ladder stitch

This stitch is also known as the slipstitch or drawing stitch (Figure 13).

With 2 hexagons side by side, insert your needle through the fold of the fabric on 1 hexagon, and take a small stitch. Insert your needle through the fold of the second hexagon and take a small stitch. Continue to the end. Pull your stitches tight to close the fabric together.

This stitch does hide the stitches better than a whipstitch in your finished piece, but it can be quite fiddly to do. I find it easier to open the hexagons up and work with them flat. You have to make sure you take very small stitches to prevent small holes in your work. This stitch does not give as firm a seam as the whipstitch.

Backstitch

This stitch (Figure 14) gives a very strong seam, but you need to be careful how deep you sew. Do not sew through the paper template.

Insert your needle from the back to the front through the fabric and take a stitch. Bring your needle back from the back to the front about 1/16″ ahead of your first stitch. Take a stitch backward to the end of the first stitch. Bring your needle from the back to the front about 1/16″ away from the end stitch. Repeat.

Figure 12: Whipstitch

Figure 13: Ladder stitch

Figure 14: Backstitch

troubleshooting

Help! The hexagons don't fit together.
Don't be afraid to adjust the fabric a bit here and there to make the hexagons align better. If they don't fit well, it is likely that the templates were not cut out properly. Next time, take more care or buy die-cut templates.

Eek! All the stitching shows.
Next time, try to choose a thread that better matches your fabric (see Needles and Thread, page 17). Or choose a different stitch type and make your stitches smaller. To fudge a bit on stitching you've already done, go over it with a fabric paint or fabric marker that matches the fabric color as closely as possible. Press your hexagons well to heat set the color. Even if the marker does not match your fabric exactly, it will disguise the stitching.

Holey moley! There are gaps between the hexagons.
Gaps will show between the hexagons if your stitches are not close enough together or tight enough. Try taking more stitches on each edge and pulling the thread a little tighter.

Removing the templates

Although historically some quilters left the paper templates in their quilts, it is a good idea to remove them. They make the fabric both stiff and heavy—not to mention what might happen when you wash the quilt!

Leave the papers in as long as possible, though, because they help to maintain the shape of your quilt. If the templates begin to bother you, remove them from all the shapes that have already been sewn into place on all sides. Carefully pull on the long thread to remove the basting stitches, as necessary, and ease the templates out. Tweezers can help with very small hexagons.

Paper templates can be reused. If they are wrinkled and creased, iron them to flatten them out again. You could even try a squirt of starch to make them crisper!

Appliquéd hexagons

In many of the projects in this book, you will appliqué the hexagons to a background fabric, either singly or in shapes composed of stitched-together hexagons. You can do this by hand or by machine. The choice is yours, but here are some factors to consider when choosing your appliqué method.

Do you want the stitches to be visible?

In hand appliqué, the stitches are hidden under the hexagon shape. In machine appliqué, the stitches are clearly visible around the edges of the appliqué shape. Consider whether you want the stitches to be a design feature of your quilt.

How do you want to quilt your finished piece?

Consider whether machine appliqué might interfere with your chosen quilting design. If so, either hand appliqué the hexagons in place and quilt over the whole top, or quilt the top and then machine or hand stitch the hexagon shapes in place. For quilting options, see Layering and Quilting (page 28).

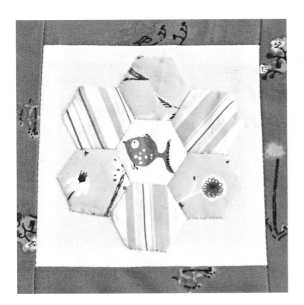

Design Note

Experiment with using different machine stitches, such as the straight stitch, zigzag, and blanket stitch, as a design feature. Use black or contrasting thread to make them really stand out.

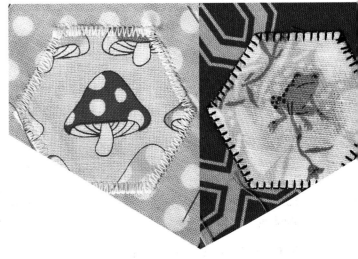

The *Giant Star Pillow* (left and on page 82) has a single hexagon appliquéd in each corner; the *Rosette Needle Book* (above left and on page 32) features hexagons stitched together into a rosette and appliquéd as a single shape.

Design Note

Machine appliqué can double as quilting. Layer your basted quilt top, batting, and backing, and then machine stitch the appliqué onto the quilt top through all the layers.

The interior rosettes on *Small Change Interactive Play Mat* (page 36) show how machine appliqué doubles as quilting along with diagonal background quilting.

What size are the hexagons?

Sometimes the decision is simply a matter of size! I recommend hand appliqué for hexagons ½˝ or smaller. With very small hexagons, any distortion in shape is more visible. I find that I have more control over the shape with hand stitching than with my machine, because I can leave the paper template in place for a longer time.

Machine stitching is better for large appliqués because managing the quilt top and hexagons by hand can be quite tricky, and also because, if you are anything like me, you just can't wait to get your quilt top finished!

HAND APPLIQUÉ

1. Remove all the paper templates from any hexagons surrounded on all sides by other hexagons. Leave the paper templates in the outer hexagons; their shape holds better with the paper templates in place.

2. Press the piece well so that the entire shape to be appliquéd is flat and the outer hexagons are better defined. This will make hand appliquéing easier.

3. Lay out the background fabric and smooth it so that there are no creases. For a large quilt, you might want to tape the background fabric in place as if you were going to layer and baste it (see Layering and Quilting, page 28).

4. Position the hexagons on top of the background fabric and pin them well or use dabs of water-soluble glue.

5. Knot the end of your thread. Hide the knot under the background fabric. Bring the needle through the background and then from the back to the top of the hexagon on the edge of the appliqué shape, right next to the fold line. Hold the appliqué and background fabric firmly with your other hand.

6. Take a small stitch through the background fabric and insert the needle through the fold of the hexagon fabric. Pull the thread through and repeat around the outside edges of the hexagon shape.

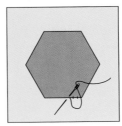

tip   Keep the stitches through the background fabric slightly inside the appliqué shape to make them less visible.

7. When only 1 side is left unstitched on any hexagon, gently remove its paper template. Use a pin to help pull the paper template out. Tuck any seam allowance back under the shape, keeping the shape of the hexagon intact. Finger-press in place and stitch the final side closed.

8. Continue around the outside edges of the appliqué shape, stitching past where you began. Take a couple of stitches in the same place to finish. Cut the threads.

MACHINE APPLIQUÉ

1. Press the hexagon appliqué well and spray with starch for extra stiffness.

2. Lay out the background fabric, smooth out any creases, and position the hexagon appliqué in place. Pin well.

3. To remove all the paper templates: Work your way around the shape, removing a pin at a time; remove the template, and then repin in place.

4. Stitch the appliqué shape in place as close to the outside edges of the shape as possible. Backstitch to secure at the start and the end.

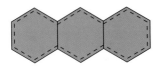

tip   Use a see-through embroidery foot to make this easier.

Design Note

Use a thread that matches the hexagon fabric if you want your stitching to blend in. Gray is a good option for multicolored fabrics. Alternatively, make a design feature of the stitching by using black thread.

Layering and quilting

When your quilt top is finished, use your preferred method to layer it for quilting. Make sure the backing and batting are 8″ larger than the quilt top *each way*.

For larger quilts, you may have to piece your batting. Lay the pieces next to each other so they are touching or even slightly overlapping, and whipstitch them together.

To secure the layers for quilting, I use straight safety pins, about 4″ to 5″ apart, and I use a spoon to close them. Curved safety pins are much easier to get through all the layers and to close, but straight ones are cheaper.

> **tip** Think about your quilting design when pinning. For example, if you want to quilt down the center of the borders, then don't place pins there!

When quilting the projects in this book, you can take advantage of the hexagon shape to create interesting patterns. In choosing a quilting design, consider how the quilt will be used. Will it be washed frequently or have to withstand a child's rough loving? In that case, you need plenty of quilting to hold it together securely. Do you want the quilting to blend into the background or to be a prominent feature?

STRAIGHT-LINE DESIGNS

Straight lines feature prominently in modern quilting. Use a walking foot, together with an adjustable bar guide, for best results. If your machine doesn't come with such a guide, you can use painter's tape to mark the lines on your quilt. This tape is great because it adheres to the quilt without leaving a sticky residue. But be careful not to stitch through the tape; it can be a devil to remove!

Straight-line quilting on *Spinning Wheels* (page 88) looks clean and modern.

Echo quilting

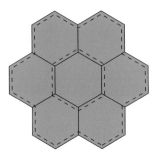

Echo quilting is a particularly good design for rosettes, hexagon borders, or anything you want to quilt using the hexagon shape. Quilt around the outline of the hexagon, both inside and outside the shape.

Echo quilting looks great with hexagons, as on the *Giant Star Pillow* (page 82).

Quilting through the hexagons

You can make all sorts of designs by quilting in straight lines through the hexagons from one side to another or even from one corner to another.

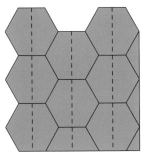

Straight line through the middle of a side with the hexagons running vertically

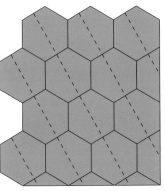

Straight line through the middle of a side with the hexagons running diagonally

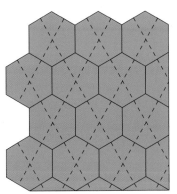

Straight lines through the middle of 2 sides to intersect diagonally

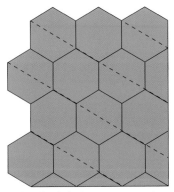

Stitch in-the-ditch along one seam and continue into the adjacent hexagon through its widest point.

Stitching goes through the hexagons on *Chevron Picnic Quilt* (page 74).

ALLOVER DESIGNS

Allover quilting designs also look great on hexagon panels. Simply lower the machine's feed dogs, use a darning foot or free-motion foot, and away you go. Treat different hexagon panels as different canvasses.

Binding

All the quilts in this book use binding strips cut on the grain with mitered corners. Use your favorite method to make the bindings.

Mix up different strips of fabric to make a scrappy binding and add depth to your quilt. For *Dropped Diamonds* (page 64), I mixed solid and print strips to break up the dullness of a solid binding without overwhelming the quilt design with a print binding.

In *Over the Rainbow* (page 107), each color block is quilted differently.

In *Stars and Stripes* (page 138), the star section is stippled and the stripes are straight-line quilted.

Experiment with stippling, loops, free-form shapes, or anything that takes your fancy.

Think outside the box and don't be afraid to mix and match different styles of quilting. Nothing says you cannot stipple some parts of your quilt and straight-line quilt other parts.

Just have fun!

rosettes

The rosette is a classic hexagon-based shape. It is made up of six hexagons stitched around a central hexagon. Rosettes are very versatile; they can be used in any element of your quilt design. Use them as stand-alone motifs as shown in the *Rosette Needle Book* (page 32), or incorporate them into your favorite blocks as featured in the *Cat Tails* quilt (page 46). Rosettes also can be sewn into strips, making them ideal for adding a little something extra to your borders. Another great way to think of rosettes is as a replacement for a star or pinwheel.

Rosette Needle Book

Designed and made by Tacha Bruecher

Hexagon size: ½˝ **Finished size:** approximately 5¾˝ × 4½˝

With all the hand sewing required to make hexagons, you will need a place to store your pins and needles. Use bits of fabric from your stash to whip up this handy needle book, and you will no longer have to search for your needle each time you want to quickly stitch a few hexagons. Slip it in your bag, and you have a cute way to make sure you and your needles are never apart!

Materials

The template pattern for the ½˝ hexagon is on page 157. Copy and cut out 7 paper templates. See Making Templates, page 18.

- 3½˝ × 3½˝ square of white solid fabric

- 7 squares 1½˝ × 1½˝ of coordinating fabrics for the hexagons

- 4˝ × 4½˝ piece of bright pink print

- 8¼˝ × 4½˝ piece of light background print

- 11¾˝ × 4½˝ piece of linen for the lining

- 11¾˝ × 3˝ piece of purple print for the inside pockets

- 1 strip 2˝ × width of coordinating fabric (40˝) for the binding

- 11¾˝ × 8˝ piece of coordinating felt

- About 3˝ of ribbon, rickrack, or trim of your choice

- 11¾˝ × 4½˝ of stiff interfacing

- 1 button ⅝˝ diameter

Cutting Instructions

From the bright pink print:

  Cut 2 strips 3½˝ × 1˝.

  Cut 2 strips 1˝ × 4½˝.

From the light background print:

  Cut 1 strip 1½˝ × 4½˝.

  Cut 1 strip 6¾˝ × 4½˝.

construction

For basic hexagon instructions, refer to Techniques (pages 18–30).

Front cover

1. Baste the 1½″ × 1½″ squares of the coordinating hexagon fabrics to the paper templates, arrange them in a rosette shape, and sew them together (Figure 1).

2. Remove the paper template from the middle hexagon. Center the rosette on the 3½″ × 3½″ white square.

3. Hand appliqué the rosette in place, removing the paper templates as you work your way around the rosette.

4. Sew the 2 bright pink 3½″ × 1″ strips to the top and the bottom of the white square. Press. Sew the 2 bright pink 1″ × 4½″ strips to the sides (Figure 2). Press.

5. Sew the light background 1½″ × 4½″ strip to the right side of the white square unit from Step 4, and sew the 6¾″ × 4½″ strip to the left side (Figure 3). Press.

Figure 1

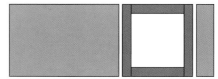

Figure 2

Figure 3

Inside pocket

1. Take the purple print strip 11¾″ × 3″ and fold over the top of the long side a scant ¼″ to the wrong side. Fold over again by ¼″. Sew along the bottom edge of the fold, as close to the edge as possible. Sew again along the top edge of the fold.

2. Place the linen lining right side up, and place the purple inside pocket piece on top, also right side up, with raw edges aligned. Sew ⅛″ in from the 3 raw edges to secure.

3. Fold the unit from Step 2 crosswise in half and press with an iron to crease. Open and fold each side in to the center crease; finger-press to crease. Sew from the bottom to the top of the pocket piece and back to the bottom of the lining on each crease (Figure 4).

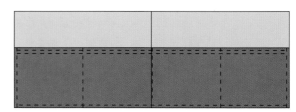

Figure 4

Put it all together

1. Sandwich the interfacing between the wrong sides of the lining piece and the front cover. Sew around the book to secure (about ⅛" in from the edges).

2. Fold the binding in half lengthwise; press. Attach the double-fold binding, using your preferred method. When hand stitching the binding to the inside of the needle book, leave a gap halfway down the right side on the inside of the back cover.

3. Make a loop with the 3" ribbon or trim. Insert the loop into the gap in the binding on the inside of the needle book with the loop facing inward, and hand stitch it firmly in place. Finish hand sewing the binding in place over the loop.

 tip The length of the ribbon loop depends on the size of your button. I used a ⅝" button and 3" of ribbon. You want the ribbon loop to sit comfortably around the button and hold the needle book closed.

4. Fold the loop to the outside of the book and close the book. Make a mark (X) where the loop meets the outside strip on the front cover (Figure 5). Sew the button on this mark.

5. Cut the felt in half lengthwise. Open the book, place a felt piece on top of the other, and center them on the book. Sew along the spine of the book, and trim the felt at each end to fit inside the binding (Figure 6).

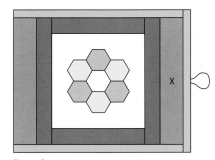

Figure 5

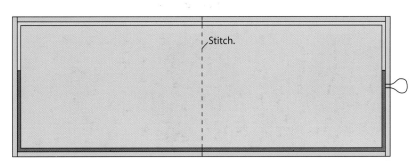

Stitch.

Figure 6

Small Change Interactive Play Mat

Designed and made by Tacha Bruecher

Hexagon sizes: ¾″, 2″ | **Finished size:** 36″ × 48″

Are you a mum-to-be, or are any of your friends expecting? With play groups, exercise classes for mums, and tummy time, a baby will spend a lot of time on the floor. A play mat made in bold colors such as red, blue, black, and white will make floor time more entertaining.

To provide a little extra fun when your little one starts to explore his or her world, add fussy-cut motifs for the border rosettes and textured fabrics for the center rosettes; hide squeakers under the center rosettes.

Materials

Template patterns for the hexagons are on page 157. Copy and cut out 182 paper templates ¾″ for the middle border rosettes and 14 paper templates 2″ for the center rosettes. See Making Templates, page 18.

- 1 yard of white solid fabric for the center panel and middle border

- 10″ × 10″ square each of 12* different black-and-white prints for the border rosettes and border rectangles

- 10″ × 10″ square each of 12* different aqua prints for the border rosettes, border rectangles, and squares

- 10″ × 10″ square each of 12* different red prints for the border rosettes, border rectangles, and squares

Design Note

Scraps of fabric such as shiny lamé, vinyl, felt, corduroy, faux fur, velvet, suede, or leather will give your child a range of sensory experiences. Try using outgrown baby clothes made of fleece or textured knits—or knit a swatch of your own! Don't be afraid to try something new. I used a silver lamé fabric in the border rosettes for added sparkle.

- 10″ × 10″ square of red solid fabric for the center rosettes

- 10″ × 10″ square of aqua solid fabric for the center rosettes

- 10″ × 10″ square of red-on-white background print for the center rosettes

- 10″ × 10″ square of aqua-on-white background print for the center rosettes

- 6 squares 2½″ × 2½″ of textured fabrics for the circles on the center rosettes

- 2 squares 4½″ × 4½″ of print fabric with a fussy-cut motif for the middle of the center rosettes

- 1¾ yards of backing fabric (44″ wide)

- 44″ × 56″ of batting

- 5 strips 2½″ × width of fabric for the binding

- 14″ × 2½″ piece of double-sided fusible web

- 2 squeakers, 2″ diameter or less (available at pet stores and online as replacement squeakers for dog toys)

*9 squares will work; 12 adds more variety.

Cutting Instructions

From the white solid fabric:
    Cut 1 rectangle 12½″ × 24½″.
    Cut 2 rectangles 6½″ × 24½″.
    Cut 2 rectangles 12½″ × 6½″.
    Cut 8 rectangles 3½″ × 6½″.
    Cut 8 squares 2″ × 2″.
    Cut 8 squares 3½″ × 3½″.

Total from the red prints:
    Cut 26 squares 2″ × 2″.
    Cut 62 rectangles 2″ × 3½″.
    Cut 8 squares 3½″ × 3½″.

Total from the aqua prints:
    Cut 26 squares 2″ × 2″.
    Cut 62 rectangles 2″ × 3½″.
    Cut 4 squares 3½″ × 3½″.

Total from the black-and-white prints:
    Cut 130 squares 2″ × 2″.
    Cut 20 rectangles 2″ × 3½″.

From the red solid fabric:
    Cut 3 squares 4½″ × 4½″.

From the aqua solid fabric:
    Cut 3 squares 4½″ × 4½″.

From the aqua-on-white print:
    Cut 3 squares 4½″ × 4½″.

From the red-on-white print:
    Cut 3 squares 4½″ × 4½″.

construction

For basic hexagon instructions, refer to Techniques (pages 18–30).

You'll piece and quilt the quilt top, and then appliqué the hexagons to the top. Press each seam as you sew for the best results.

Play mat layout

Piecing and quilting

The quilt top is made up of 4 Block A's, 2 Block B's, 2 Block C's, and a center rectangle.

BLOCK A

Make 4. Block size (unfinished) is 12½″ × 12½″.

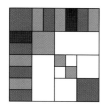

Block A

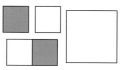

Figure 1

Figure 2

Figure 3

Figure 4

1. To make a block, refer to Figure 1 and sew 2 aqua print squares 2″ × 2″ and 2 white squares 2″ × 2″ into a four-patch unit. Sew the four-patch unit to a white square 3½″ × 3½″.

2. Sew 1 white strip 6½″ × 3½″ to the top of the unit from Step 1 (Figure 2). Sew a white square 3½″ × 3½″ to a red square 3½″ × 3½″, and sew this to the bottom of the unit as shown.

3. Sew an aqua print square 3½″ × 3½″ to a white rectangle 3½″ × 6½″. Sew this to the left side of the unit from Step 2 (Figure 3).

4. Select 12 rectangles 2″ × 3½″ (2 black/white and the rest a mix of red and aqua prints). Arrange and sew them into 2 strips of 6 "coins" (rectangles). Sew a coin strip to the left side of the unit from Step 3. Sew a red square 3½″ × 3½″ to the end of the other coin strip. Sew this coin strip to the top of the block (Figure 4).

5. Repeat Steps 1–4 to make 4 blocks.

BLOCK B

Make 2. Block size (unfinished) is 12½″ × 12½″.

Block B

1. To make a block, select 16 rectangles 3½″ × 2″ (2 black/white and the rest a mix of red and aqua prints). Arrange and sew the rectangles in 2 strips of 8 rectangles. Sew these strips to the long sides of the white rectangle 12½″ × 6½″ (Figure 5).

2. Repeat Step 1 to make 2 blocks.

Figure 5

BLOCK C

Make 2. Block size (unfinished) is 12½″ × 24½″.

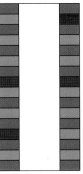

Block C

1. To make a block, select 32 rectangles 2″ × 3½″ (4 black/white and the rest a mix of red and aqua prints). Arrange and sew the rectangles in 2 strips of 16 rectangles. Sew these strips to the sides of the white rectangle 6½″ × 24½″ (Figure 6).

2. Repeat Step 1 to make 2 of these blocks.

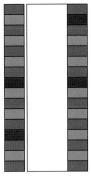

Figure 6

QUILT TOP ASSEMBLY

1. Refer to Figure 7 to sew a Block C to each long side of the 12½″ × 24½″ white rectangle.

2. Sew a Block A to each side of each Block B, making sure to orient the blocks as shown. Sew these A/B sections to the top and bottom of the center panel from Step 1.

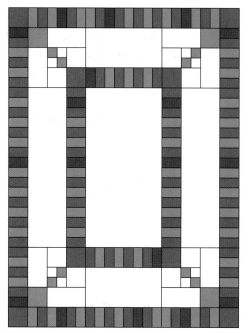

Figure 7

QUILTING

1. Cut the backing to size, and layer and baste the backing, batting, and quilt top.

2. Use painter's tape to mark diagonal lines (about 1⅛″–1¼″ apart) across the quilt's center panel, and quilt.

3. Quilt straight lines along the edges of the pieced borders with parallel lines of stitching inside, and quilt diagonally through the corner blocks.

Hexagon appliqués

In the center panel, 2 hexagons conceal squeakers; other hexagons have circles of textured fabrics in their centers. Refer to Appliquéd Hexagons (page 24) for general instructions.

CENTER HEXAGONS

1. Take the 3 squares 4½″ × 4½″ of aqua solid fabric, 3 of red solid fabric, and 2 of the fussy-cut fabric. Baste them to the 2″ hexagon templates. The fussy-cut hexagons are the centers of the rosettes.

2. For the texture-centered hexagons, draw and cut out 6 circles (2″ diameter) from the fusible web.

3. Follow the manufacturer's instructions to fuse the fusible web circles to the wrong side of the 6 squares 2½″ × 2½″ of textured fabric. Cut out the fabric circles.

tip Be careful when fusing the web to the textured squares. Some fabrics such as lamé or even felt can be heat sensitive. Place another piece of fabric between the iron and the scrap.

4. Take the 3 squares 4½″ × 4½″ of the red-on-white print and 3 of the aqua-on-white print. Peel off the paper backing from the fabric circles from Step 3, center them on the print squares, and fuse them in place.

5. Sew around the circles using a zigzag stitch to secure them in place.

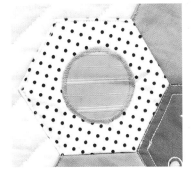

tip The closer together the zigzag stitches, the better the circle is secured in place. Stitch around the circle twice for an even better result.

6. Baste these textured-center squares to the remaining 2″ hexagon templates.

7. Arrange and sew the 2″ hexagons into 2 rosettes. Each rosette has a fussy-cut hexagon in the center, plus 3 plain hexagons and 3 hexagons with textured circles.

8. Remove the paper template from the center hexagon in each rosette.

9. Refer to the play mat layout to arrange the rosettes on the center white panel of the quilt. Slip a squeaker under the center hexagon of each rosette and pin around the squeaker to secure the central hexagon in place.

10. Work your way around each hexagon in the rosettes, removing the paper templates and repinning the hexagons in place.

11. Stitch slightly inside the center hexagon and then again ¼″ in from the edge. Stitch around the whole rosette about ⅛″ in from the edge.

BORDER HEXAGONS

1. Select 182 squares 2″ × 2″ (130 black/white, 26 aqua print, and 26 red print). Baste the squares to the ¾″ hexagon templates. Arrange and sew them in groups of 7, in a rosette shape.

2. Refer to the play mat layout (page 39) to arrange and sew the rosettes into 2 strips of 5 and 2 strips of 8. Press.

3. Remove the paper templates from all the center hexagons in the rosettes, and center both 5-rosette strips on the white borders along the short sides of the quilt. Pin in place.

4. Center both 8-rosette strips on the white borders along the long sides of the quilt. Pin in place.

5. Go around the strips a hexagon at a time, unpinning, removing the paper template, and then repinning in place.

6. Stitch the strips in place, sewing as close to the outside edges as possible.

Finishing

Use your favorite method to bind your quilt using the 5 strips 2½″ × width of fabric.

Design Note

Arrange the hexagons so that each rosette is predominantly black and white with the odd red and aqua print to add contrast.

Cat Tails Quilt

Designed and made by Tacha Bruecher

Hexagon size: 1½″ | **Finished size:** 70″ × 92″

My girls are just crazy about cats. So when I found a pair of Munki Munki pajamas with cats on them, I just knew they would make the most perfect quilt for my daughters!

Because the cat motifs I cut from the pajamas are quite small, I chose simple hexagon rosettes to frame them. I coupled the rosette blocks with scrappy string blocks. String quilts are a popular way to use up scraps—all those bits and pieces you have stuffed into boxes under the bed! I raided my pink, red, yellow, and orange scrap bins; I only had to add the brown strips to contrast the midtone colors.

Materials

The template pattern for 1½″ hexagon is on page 157. Copy and cut out 140 paper templates. See Making Templates, page 18.

- 5 yards of solid white fabric

- 1¼ yards of brown print (2 yards for continuous borders)

- 1 fat quarter *each* of 6 different red prints

- 1 fat quarter *each* of 4 different yellow prints

- 1 fat quarter *each* of 5 different orange prints

- 20 squares 3½″ × 3½″ of fussy-cut motifs (optional, for the rosette centers)

- ⅝ yard *each* of 5 different pink prints

- 5¾ yards of backing fabric*

- 9 strips 2½″ × width of fabric for binding

- 78″ × 100″ piece of batting

- 80 squares 8½″ × 8½″ of freezer paper for blocks

A money-saving alternative is to use leftover fabric strips to make a series of Log Cabin blocks for the back of your quilt, as shown in Finishing (page 53). You'll make a feature of your quilt back as well!

Cutting Instructions

From the white solid fabric:

Cut 2 strips 3½˝ × 86½˝.

Cut 2 strips 3½˝ × 70½˝.

Cut 2 strips 1½˝ × 64½˝.

Cut 40 squares 8½˝ × 8½˝.

Cut 80 strips 1¼˝ × 12½˝.

From the brown print:

Cut 2 strips 2½˝ × 64½˝.

Cut 80 strips 1˝ × 11¼˝.

From the red, yellow, orange, and pink prints*:

Cut about 240 strips 11¼˝ × 1˝ to 2˝ wide.

Cut about 100 strips 8˝ × 1˝ to 2˝ wide.

Cut about 200 strips 6˝ × 1˝ to 2˝ wide.

Cut 140 squares 3½˝ × 3½˝ for the rosettes.

*You may need more or fewer strips for string piecing, depending on how wide you cut them and how many you use per block. For the squares, if you are using a motif such as the cat in the center of the rosettes, cut 20 squares 3½˝ × 3½˝ from your motif fabric and 120 squares from the prints.

s 18–30).

arters.

xagon

Quilt layout

Design Note

If you want to use fussy-cut motifs for
this project, look for motifs about 2″ × 2″
square. You will need 20. When buying
fabric, take into account the number of
motifs per length of fabric and how widely
apart they are spaced. The easiest way to
work out how much fabric you will need
is to make a plastic template (see Making
Templates, page 18). Take this template
to the fabric store, try it out on the fabric,
and then measure the yardage you need
for 20 motifs. If you buy your fabric online,
you could email the shop owner and ask to
have someone measure the fabric for you.

String piecing

The string quarter-block units (unfinished) are 8½″ × 8½″. Each string quarter-block unit is made in 2 sections. One side of the central white strip is pieced with color strips; the other is pieced with a single brown strip and a white triangle.

1. On the dull side of each of the 80 freezer-paper squares, draw a line along the diagonal from corner to corner.

2. Press a white fabric strip 1¼″ × 12½″ so that it is straight.

3. Center the diagonal line of a freezer-paper square over the white strip (Figure 1). With the shiny side against the fabric, press briefly with your iron. The freezer paper will stick to the fabric strip. Repeat for all the freezer-paper squares and white 1¼″ × 12½″ strips.

4. Cut all the solid white 8½″ × 8½″ squares in half diagonally to make 80 triangles.

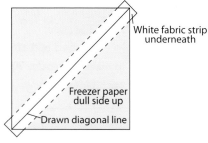

Figure 1

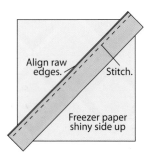

Figure 2

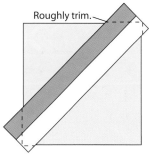

Figure 3

> **tip** When stitching through the freezer paper, use an old needle on your machine; the paper will blunt the needle. Reduce your stitch length—because the more times the paper is perforated by the needle, the easier it is to tear away. When you're finished, store the needle clearly marked, "Use for paper sewing only!"

5. To make a quarter-block unit, lay a 11¼″ color strip right side down on the white strip from Step 3, matching raw edges as shown. Sew in place through the strips *and* the freezer paper (Figure 2). Note that this first strip fits exactly, so place it carefully.

6. Open up the strips, press, and roughly trim the ends using the freezer paper as a guide (Figure 3).

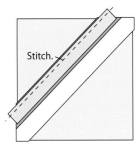

Figure 4

Figure 5

Figure 6

7. Fold the freezer paper back behind the strips (do not remove). Place another color strip on top, right sides together and matching raw edges, and sew through just the strips, not the freezer paper (Figure 4). Press.

8. Continue sewing on strips and pressing until the string-pieced half of the freezer-paper square is covered (Figure 5). Periodically unfold the freezer paper back against the strips as you stitch to check that the strips cover the area of the freezer paper.

9. With the freezer paper unfolded and against the fabric strips, place a brown strip on the other side of the first white strip, right sides together and raw edges aligned. Sew in place through the strips *and* the freezer paper (Figure 6). Press.

10. Fold the freezer paper under. Place a white 8½˝ triangle on the brown strip, right sides together and matching raw edges, and sew through just the fabric, not the freezer paper (Figure 7).

11. Press. Then fold the freezer paper back against the fabric, and press the quarter-block unit so that the freezer paper sticks to the fabric. Trim the quarter-block unit to 8½˝ × 8½˝, using the freezer paper as a guide (Figure 8).

12. Fold the freezer paper on one side of the white center strip, along the stitching. Crease firmly and tear away. Repeat for the other side and then remove the center strip of freezer paper.

13. Repeat Steps 5–12 to make 80 quarter-block units.

> **tip** To minimize damage to your stitching when removing the freezer paper, press down firmly on the stitching with one hand, and use the other hand to carefully tear the paper away.

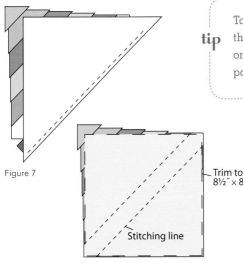

Figure 7

Figure 8

Hexagon rosettes

Make 20 hexagon rosettes.

1. Baste the 140 print and fussy cut 3½″ × 3½″ squares to the hexagon paper templates.

2. Arrange and sew the hexagons in groups of 7, in a rosette shape, with the fussy-cut motif in the center. Spray with starch and press. Put these aside.

tip You can use spray starch to help your hexagons maintain their shape. After spraying, place a piece of clean muslin between your iron and the hexagon rosette to prevent starch from transferring to the iron.

Block assembly

Make 20 string blocks. The blocks (unfinished) are 16½″ × 16½″.

1. Match 2 string quarter-block units right sides together. Line up the white and brown strips and pin in place. Sew together. Repeat with another pair of quarter-block units, making sure they are oriented as shown in Figure 9.

2. Press the seams open. Pin together the 2 sets of quarter-block units so that the white strips, brown strips, and middle seams align, and sew together to make a block of 4.

3. Repeat Steps 1 and 2 to make 20 string blocks.

4. Remove the templates from the center hexagon in each rosette. Center each rosette on a string block and pin in place.

5. Remove the hexagon basting and templates from the outer hexagons and repin in place.

6. Stitch the rosettes in place, sewing as close to the edges as possible.

Figure 9

Figure 10

Design Note

If you will be using an allover quilting design, you might want to appliqué the rosettes after the quilt top has been assembled and quilted.

Quilt top assembly

1. Refer to the quilt layout (page 49) to sew the string blocks into 5 rows of 4 blocks each. Press as you stitch. Sew the rows together. Press.

2. Sew the borders to the quilt top in the following order:

   1½″ × 64½″ white border to the top and the bottom of the quilt top

   2½″ × 64½″ brown border to the top and the bottom of the quilt top

   3½″ × 86½″ white border to the sides of the quilt top

   3½″ × 70½″ white border to the top and bottom of the quilt top

tip The diagonal strip blocks can stretch because of all the seams. To prevent stretching, use plenty of pins to attach the borders to the quilt before sewing.

Finishing

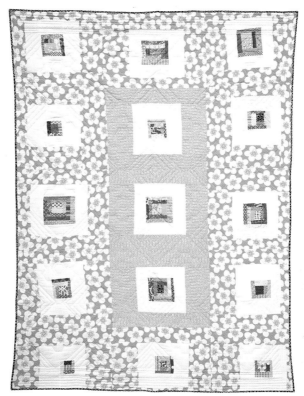

Back of *Cat Tails* quilt

You can use a single fabric for the entire backing, or sew any leftover strips into Log Cabin blocks and use these as part of your backing fabric. I made Log Cabin blocks of differing sizes and used 2 different backing fabrics to sash the blocks.

1. Cut out or piece the backing. Layer and baste the backing, batting, and quilt top.

2. Quilt as desired. I echo quilted the hexagon rosettes inside and just outside of the group, and then quilted concentric squares in the string blocks.

3. Use your favorite binding method to sew together the 2½″ binding strips and bind the quilt.

diamonds

Although rosettes are probably the best-known hexagon shape, the diamond comes in a close second. One of my favorite diamond patterns is the argyle pattern, in which diagonal lines of hexagons crisscross large diamond shapes composed of hexagons. As you can see from the *Argyle* quilt (page 56), the hexagon diamond shape lends itself perfectly to this design.

You can create hexagon diamonds by stitching together a center of either one or four hexagons and adding concentric rings of diamonds around them.

Make monotone diamonds with hexagons that are different values of the same color. For alternative designs, stitch hexagons of different colors around the central hexagons to mimic a Log Cabin, or break the diamond shape apart to form chevrons, as in the *Chevron Picnic Quilt (page 74)*, or even triangles.

Argyle Quilt

Designed and made by Tacha Bruecher

Hexagon size: 1½˝ | **Finished size:** 80½˝ × 106½˝

Argyle patterns were traditionally masculine and were found primarily on socks and golf attire—and kilts! But the pattern can be made more feminine, depending on the colors used.

In this quilt, the argyle patterns are combined with pieced triangle blocks to make a bold, graphic statement. Although I designed this quilt for an older child or young adult, I think it would be a big hit with all ages! For younger children, try adding lots of fussy-cut motifs for an "I Spy" quilt.

Materials

The template pattern for the 1½˝ hexagon is on page 157. Copy and cut out 445 paper templates. See Making Templates, page 18.

- 8 yards of white solid fabric *or* 1⅝ yards of white solid broadcloth* (108˝ wide) and 2½ yards of white solid (40˝ wide) for center panel and borders

- 3¼ yards of brown print for the crisscross hexagons and borders

- 20 fat quarters of coordinating prints for the hexagons, triangle blocks, and scrappy borders (see Design Note).

- 11 strips 2½˝ × width of fabric for the binding

- 7⅝ yards of backing fabric

- 89˝ × 115˝ of batting

- 9½˝ × 12½˝ template plastic

*With wide fabric, you can avoid piecing the white center panel. But if you do piece, the center seam will be hidden beneath the hexagons.

Design Note

If you want each large diamond to be monotone like those shown, you will need 4 fat quarters of the same color for each diamond.

construction

For basic hexagon instructions, refer to Techniques (pages 18–30).

Cutting Instructions

From the white solid fabric:

  Cut 2 strips 2½″ × 81″.

  Cut 2 strips 2¾″ × 81″.

  Cut 20 rectangles 5½″ × 14½″.

From the brown print:

  Cut 2 strips 2½″ × 94½″.

  Cut 2 strips 2½″ × 77″.

  Cut 265 squares 3½″ × 3½″.

From each fat quarter:

  Cut 6 strips 2″ × 12½″. (Cut these first, parallel to the shorter side of the fat quarter, for the triangle borders.)

  Cut 9 squares 3½″ × 3½″ for the hexagons.

  Cut the remaining fabric into 2½″-wide pieces in a variety of lengths for the scrappy borders.

Quilt layout

White center panel

1. If you are piecing this panel, cut the 9 yards into 2 lengths of 2⅔ yards and put the remainder aside for now. Sew the 2⅔ yard pieces together lengthwise. Press.

2. Measure 26½" away from the center seam on both sides, and cut out the center panel so that it measures 53" wide.

3. Trim the length of the panel to 90½" by squaring up and trimming from both the top and the bottom of the panel.

Note: If you are using 108"-wide broadcloth, trim the 1⅝-yard piece to 53" × 90½".

Hexagons

1. Baste the brown and the fat quarter squares 3½" × 3½" to the hexagon paper templates.

2. Arrange and sew the fat quarter hexagons into 20 diamonds consisting of 9 hexagons each (Figure 1). Press.

3. Take 4 of the diamonds and 25 brown hexagons, and arrange and sew into a larger diamond shape with the brown hexagons forming a cross between the small diamonds. Repeat to make 5 large cross shapes. Press. Sew the 5 cross shapes together (Figure 2). Press.

4. Sew 72 brown hexagons into 2 strips of 36 hexagons, and sew 12 brown hexagons into 4 strips of 3 hexagons.

5. Arrange and sew 56 brown hexagons into 8 V shapes of 7 hexagons each (Figure 3).

6. Arrange and sew together the different parts to make the hexagon panel (Figure 4). Press.

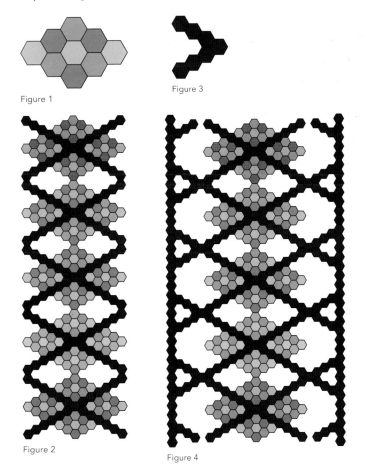

Figure 1

Figure 3

Figure 2

Figure 4

Triangle blocks

Here, you will make your own template to use for cutting isosceles triangles from pieced strips. Make 20 blocks.

1. Arrange and sew the 120 fat quarter strips 2″ × 12½″ into 20 units of 6 strips (Figure 5). Press the seams.

2. To make your template, draw a rectangle measuring 9″ × 12″ on a piece of paper. Mark the center point along one of the 9″ sides, and draw a line from the corners of the opposite 9″ side to the center point to create an isosceles triangle. Use your ruler to measure ¼″ around the triangle on all sides to add the ¼″ seam allowances (Figure 6). Trace the triangle onto the template plastic and cut it out.

> **tip** You may have to tape 2 pieces of paper together to draw a large enough rectangle.

3. Use the template to cut out a triangle from each of the 20 strip units (Figure 7).

4. Place 2 white 5½″ × 14½″ rectangles right sides facing, and cut in half diagonally. Repeat for the remaining white triangles. Sew the white triangles to either side of the pieced-strip triangles. Note that you need a white triangle from each paired white rectangle. Press the seams as you go. Trim this block to 9½″ × 12½″ (Figure 8).

5. Refer to the quilt layout (page 58) to arrange and sew the blocks into 2 strips of 10 blocks each.

Figure 5

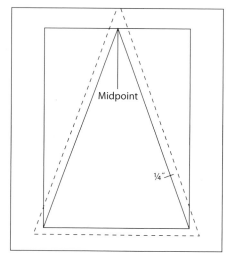

Figure 6

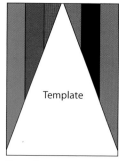

Figure 7

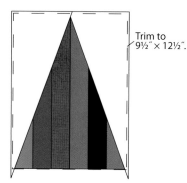

Figure 8

Center panel assembly

1. Refer to the quilt layout to sew the 2 triangle strips to either side of the white center panel. Press.

2. Lay the center panel on a flat surface, smooth out any wrinkles, and center the hexagon panel on top of the white panel.

 tip Spray the hexagon panel with starch to make sure that it doesn't lose its shape.

3. Line up the edges of the hexagon panel with the white panel and triangle border seams so that the points of the hexagons are just touching the seams on both sides of the white panel. When you are happy with the position of the hexagon panel, pin it in place in key spots.

4. Go around the hexagon panel, taking out a pin at a time, removing your basting threads, easing out all the paper templates, and then repinning in place. Because you pressed and starched the hexagons, the fabric should keep its shape without the paper templates.

5. Sew around the hexagon panel as close to the edge of the outside hexagons as you can, to secure them in place.

6. If you wish, cut out the white fabric behind each hexagon diamond to reduce bulk. Trim the overhanging hexagons at the top and bottom in line with the white panel.

Borders

1. Sew the 2 brown strips 2½″ × 77″ to the top and bottom of the quilt. Press.

2. Sew the 2 brown strips 2½″ × 94½″ to the sides of the quilt. Press.

3. Sew the 2½″-wide scraps from the fat quarters together to make 2 strips 2½″ × 81″. Press.

4. Sew a white strip 2½″ × 81″ and a white strip 2¾″ × 81″ to either side of each pieced strip from Step 3 along the 81″ edges (Figure 9). Press.

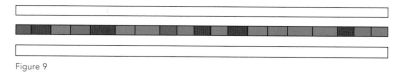

Figure 9

5. Sew these pieced strips to the top and the bottom of the quilt, placing the wider white strips toward the outside edges. Press.

Finishing

1. Layer and baste the backing, batting, and quilt top.

2. Quilt as desired. The angular shape of the diamonds and triangles lends itself well to straight-line quilting. I quilted straight lines through the diamonds to echo the argyle design. I also used straight lines to outline the triangles and to quilt through the borders.

3. Use your favorite method to sew the 2½″ binding strips together and bind the quilt.

Dropped Diamonds Quilt

Designed and made by Tacha Bruecher and longarm quilted by Nina Reingruber of http://1001quilt.de

Hexagon size: 2″	Finished size: 100″ × 108″

Don't be afraid to cut off hexagon shapes to make more interesting designs. *Dropped Diamonds* has only one complete diamond. The rest are partial diamonds, making the design asymmetrical and modern.

Notice that the diamonds are formed using concentric rings of hexagons. Each ring is made from one color. Pepper your diamond shapes with rings of contrasting hexagons; in my quilt I used a deep pink. You could even imitate the improv look by using a hexagon or two of a different color in each ring of the diamond shape.

To give this design a more modern twist, I paired the hexagon diamonds panel with an arrow border. The half-square arrow shapes echo the corners of the diamonds in the main design and make the quilt more striking.

There is a lot going on in this quilt, so it was tempting to use a plain solid binding, but that left the quilt looking a bit flat. Instead I went with a scrappy binding of green print and green solid.

Design Note

Cut the hexagons needed for each diamond ring from the 1½-yard cuts of fabric. Each cut yields at least 80 hexagons, which is enough to make either 3 large rings, such as 36 + 28 + 12, or 4 rings, such as 4 + 12 + 33 + 20. This gives you a little extra to play with in making your quilt. *The ring sizes and placement are up to you.* Have fun choosing the fabric for each ring, and remember that you can always make a few scrappy rings if you haven't got enough of one print to make a complete ring.

Materials

The template pattern for the 2″ hexagon is on page 157. Copy and cut out 765 paper templates. See Making Templates, page 18.

- 4¾ yards of white solid fabric for hexagons, arrow blocks, and borders*

- 1½ yards *each* of at least 7 coordinating prints for hexagons and arrow blocks (I used 9)

- 1½ yards of contrasting print (I used pink) for hexagons, arrow blocks, and corners

- 3 yards of dark blue print (2 yards if you piece the long borders) for hexagons, arrow blocks, and borders*

- 12 strips 2½″ × width of fabric for binding**

- 108″ × 116″ of backing fabric (9⅛ yards, or 3⅜ yards of extra-wide 108″ fabric)

- 108″ × 116″ piece of batting

Cut the borders lengthwise from the fabric.

**Use a single fabric or cut strips from various fabrics.*

Cutting Instructions

From the white solid fabric:

Cut 144 squares 3½″ × 3½″ for the arrow blocks.

Cut 135 squares 4½″ × 4½″ for the hexagons.

Cut 2 strips 2¼″ × 87″.

Cut 2 strips 2¼″ × 90½″.

Cut 2 strips 2½″ × 100½″.

From the pink print:

Cut 4 squares 5½″ × 5½″ for the corners.

From the dark blue print:

Cut 2 strips 2½″ × 100½″.

In total, from the pink, dark blue, and coordinating prints:

For the arrow blocks:

Cut 72 lots of 2 squares 3½″ × 3½″. (Cut 2 squares from one print fabric, and then cut 2 squares from another print fabric; do this to make 72 lots of 2 squares.)

For the hexagons that form the diamonds, where the innermost ring is made from 4 hexagons, the next ring has 12 hexagons, and so on. (See Hexagon Panel, page 69, for placement.):

Cut 1 lot of 36 squares 4½″ × 4½″. (Cut 36 squares from the same fabric.)

Cut 1 lot of 33 squares 4½″ × 4½″.

Cut 2 lots of 31 squares 4½″ × 4½. (Cut 31 squares from one print fabric, and then cut 31 squares from another print fabric.)

Cut 2 lots of 28 squares 4½″ × 4½″.

Cut 2 lots of 27 squares 4½″ × 4½″.

Cut 2 lots of 21 squares 4½″ × 4½″.

Cut 4 lots of 20 squares 4½″ × 4½″.

Cut 3 lots of 17 squares 4½″ × 4½″.

Cut 3 lots of 13 squares 4½″ × 4½″.

Cut 4 lots of 12 squares 4½″ × 4½″.

Cut 1 lot of 11 squares 4½″ × 4½″.

Cut 5 lots of 9 squares 4½″ × 4½″.

Cut 2 lots of 7 squares 4½″ × 4½″.

Cut 4 lots of 5 squares 4½″ × 4½″.

Cut 7 lots of 4 squares 4½″ × 4½″.

Cut 2 lots of 3 squares 4½″ × 4½″.

Cut 1 lot of 2 squares 4½″ × 4½″.

Cut 3 lots of 1 square 4½″ × 4½″.

construction

Refer to Techniques (pages 18–30) for basic hexagon instructions.

Quilt layout

Hexagon panel

1. Baste all the white and print squares 4½″ × 4½″ to the 2″ hexagon templates.

2. Arrange and sew the print hexagons into diamonds as shown in Figure 1. Make 1 each of Blocks A, C, E, G, H, and I. Make 2 each of Blocks B, D, and F. Starting with the innermost ring, the numbers of hexagons per ring are shown below each block illustration. These correspond to the numbers of squares cut in each lot for the hexagons.

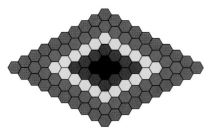

Block A

4 hexagons + 12 hexagons + 20 hexagons + 28 hexagons + 36 hexagons

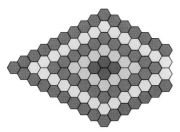

Block B

4 hexagons + 12 hexagons + 20 hexagons + 27 hexagons + 31 hexagons

Make 2.

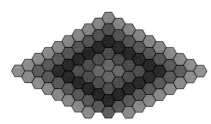

Block C

4 hexagons + 12 hexagons + 20 hexagons + 28 hexagons + 33 hexagons

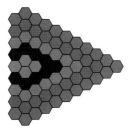

Block D

4 hexagons + 9 hexagons + 13 hexagons + 17 hexagons + 21 hexagons

Make 2.

Block E

1 hexagon + 5 hexagons + 9 hexagons + 13 hexagons + 17 hexagons

Block F

1 hexagon + 5 hexagons + 9 hexagons

Make 2.

Block G

3 hexagons + 7 hexagons + 11 hexagons

Block H

3 hexagons + 5 hexagons + 7 hexagons

Block I

2 hexagons + 4 hexagons

Figure 1

3. Arrange and sew the white hexagons into 4 strips of 10 hexagons, 1 strip of 7 hexagons, 3 strips of 6 hexagons, 1 strip of 14 hexagons, 1 strip of 23 hexagons, and 1 strip of 30 hexagons. You should have 3 white hexagons left over.

4. Refer to Figure 2 to sew the diamonds and white strips together as follows to form diagonal rows:

> Row 2—1 white hexagon, Block D, strip of 10 white hexagons, Block E
>
> Row 4—1 white hexagon, Block D, strip of 10 white hexagons, Block A, strip of 10 white hexagons, Block B, strip of 6 hexagons, Block I
>
> Row 6—Block H, strip of 7 white hexagons, Block C, strip of 10 white hexagons, Block B, strip of 6 white hexagons, Block F
>
> Row 8—Block G, strip of 6 white hexagons, Block F

5. Refer to Figure 2 to sew the diagonal rows together including the following:

> Row 1—1 white hexagon
>
> Row 3—strip of 23 white hexagons
>
> Row 5—strip of 30 white hexagons
>
> Row 7—strip of 14 white hexagons

6. Open up the seam allowances on the hexagons at the top and the bottom of the panel and press. Trim the panel to 87″ × 87″. Remove the hexagon basting and paper templates.

tip Two adjacent hexagons measure 6″ across. To establish the width of the panel, mark 14 repetitions of 2 hexagons and then measure 1½″ from the start and end of the repetitions.

4″ 2″

7. Sew the 2¼″ × 87″ white strips to the top and bottom of the quilt top. Press. Sew the 2¼″ × 90½″ white strips to the sides of the quilt top. Press.

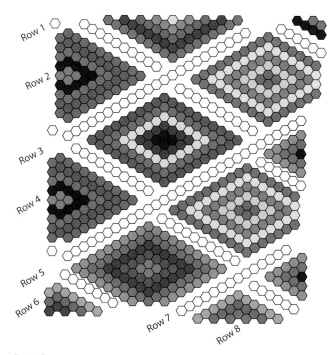

Row 1
Row 2
Row 3
Row 4
Row 5
Row 6
Row 7
Row 8

Figure 2

Arrow blocks

Half-square triangle units form these arrow blocks used in the border designs. These arrow blocks (unfinished) measure 5½″ × 5½″. Make 72.

1. Select a pair of print squares 3½″ × 3½″ and a pair of white squares 3½″ × 3½″, and draw a diagonal line on the wrong side of each white square. Pair each white square with a print square, right sides together, and sew ¼″ away on both sides of the diagonal line (Figure 3). Cut along the centerline. Open, press, and trim to 3″ × 3″. Repeat for all the pairs of print and white 3½″ × 3½″ squares.

2. Arrange and sew together the resulting 4 half-square triangles to create an arrow shape (Figure 4), pressing as you go.

3. Repeat Steps 1 and 2 to make 72 arrow blocks measuring 5½″ × 5½″ unfinished.

4. Arrange and sew the arrow blocks in 8 strips of 9 blocks each. Sew these strips in pairs, rotating a strip in each pair 180° (Figure 5).

Quilt top assembly

1. Refer to the quilt layout (page 68) to sew 2 of the arrow block strips to the top and bottom of the quilt top. Press.

2. Sew a pink square 5½″ × 5½″ to each end of the remaining 18-block strips. Press. Sew these strips to the sides of the quilt top.

3. Sew the white 2½″ × 100½″ strips to the top and bottom of the quilt top. Press.

4. Sew the print 2½″ × 100½″ strips to the top and bottom of the quilt top. Press.

Draw line.
Stitch ¼″ from line.
¼″

Figure 3

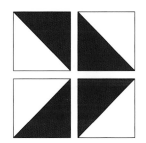

Figure 4

Figure 5

Finishing

1. Layer and baste the backing, batting, and quilt top.

2. Quilt as desired. This quilt was longarm quilted by Nina Reingruber of http://1001quilt.de. I used the fabric line Modern Meadow by Joel Dewberry for this quilt, so we decided to continue the idea of a modern meadow in the quilting. Each diamond is filled with a flower, and the white hexagon borders are quilted with a leaf pattern.

3. Use your favorite method to sew the 2½″ binding strips together and bind the quilt. You can piece together different fabrics for a scrappy binding as I did, or use a single fabric.

Chevron Picnic Quilt

Designed and made by Tacha Bruecher

Hexagon size: 1½″ | **Finished size:** 76″ × 70″

Cut diamonds in half to create chevrons that you can arrange in a zigzag design. This is a great way to show off small amounts of fabrics from your stash and to create a fantastic picnic quilt large enough for quite a spread!

Each V in this quilt requires, at the most, only 11 hexagons. Perhaps you have a pile of fat quarters from your favorite fabric line that you don't know what to do with, or lots of reasonably large scraps from other projects. This is the perfect way to use them up. Use any leftovers from the fat quarters to make the Flying Geese border and the scrappy strips that separate the three chevron panels.

Materials

The template pattern for the 1½″ hexagon is on page 157. Copy and cut out 479 paper templates. See Making Templates, paage 18.

- 2 yards of cream solid fabric
- 2 yards of brown solid fabric
- 26 fat quarters of coordinating prints
- 4⅞ yards of backing
- 8 strips 2½″ × width of fabric for binding
- 78″ × 84″ of batting

Cutting Instructions

From the cream solid:

Cut 4 strips 2¾″ × 65½″.

Cut 260 squares 2½″ × 2½″ for the Flying Geese border.

Cut 8 strips 1½″ × 2½″ for the 4 corners.

Cut 8 strips 1½″ × 4½″ for the 4 corners.

From the brown solid:

Cut 2 strips 2″ × 62½″.

Cut 2 strips 2½″ × 65½″.

Cut 4 strips 1½″ × 65½″.

Cut 4 strips 1¼″ × 65½″.

Cut 4 squares 2½″ × 2½″ for the 4 corners.

In total, from the fat quarters:

For the hexagons:

Cut 36 lots of 11 squares 3½″ × 3½″. (Cut 11 squares from the same print, and then cut 11 more squares from a second print; repeat to make 36 lots of 11 squares. Some prints will repeat.)

Cut 2 lots of 10 squares 3½″ × 3½″.

Cut 1 lot of 9 squares 3½″ × 3½″.

Cut 1 lot of 8 squares 3½″ × 3½″.

Cut 2 lots of 7 squares 3½″ × 3½″.

Cut 2 lots of 6 squares 3½″ × 3½″.

Cut 1 lot of 5 squares 3½″ × 3½″.

Cut 1 lot of 4 squares 3½″ × 3½″.

Cut 2 lots of 3 squares 3½″ × 3½″.

Cut 2 lots of 2 squares 3½″ × 3½″.

Cut 1 square 3½″ × 3½″.

For the Flying Geese border:

Cut 130 rectangles 2½″ × 4½″.

For the scrappy strips:

Cut the leftover scraps into pieces 2″ wide for the 2 scrappy strips.

Design Note

This quilt has 51 V's; in each V, all the hexagons are made from the same print. Some are complete V's containing 11 hexagons, and others are partial V's containing from 1 hexagon to 10 hexagons. When cutting the squares from the fat quarters, keep in mind that the leftover fabric will be used for the Flying Geese border and the scrappy strips. Distribute the squares for the hexagons among the fat quarters to have a variety of prints remaining for the Flying Geese border.

construction

For basic hexagon instructions, refer to Techniques (pages 18–30).

Quilt layout

Hexagon panels

1. Baste the 479 print 3½″ × 3½″ squares to the hexagon templates.

2. Arrange and sew the 36 groups of 11 hexagons of the same print into full V's (Figure 1).

3. Arrange and sew these 36 V's into 3 groups of 12 (Figure 2). Turn 1 of the panels 180° to face the opposite direction. This will be the center panel.

4. Sew together groups of 10, 9, 8, 7, 6, 5, 4, and 3 hexagons of the same print into partial V's (Figure 3).

5. Sew the partial V's to the 3 panels of full V's as shown in Figure 4.

6. Press the panels. Remove the basting thread and hexagon templates. *Open up the seam allowances on the outer hexagons and press again.* Trim each panel to 13½″ × 65½″.

7. Sew the leftover 2″-wide scraps into 2 strips 2″ × 65½″. Press.

8. Sew each cream strip 2¾″ × 65½″ between a brown strip 1¼″ × 65½″ and a brown strip 1½″ × 65½″ along the long edges (Figure 5). Then press.

9. Sew the cream/brown sections to either side of the scrappy strips so that the narrower brown strips are next to the scrappy strip (Figure 5). Press.

10. Refer to the quilt layout (page 76) to sew the hexagon panels and the scrappy strip sections together in rows. Press.

11. Sew the brown strips 2½″ × 65½″ to the top and bottom of the quilt top. Sew the brown strips 2″ × 62½″ to the sides of the quilt top. Press the seams.

The quilt top measures 62½″ × 68½″ (unfinished).

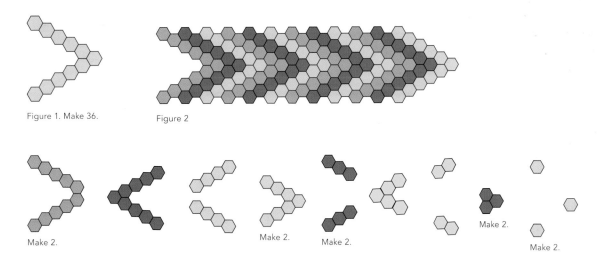

Figure 1. Make 36.

Figure 2

Make 2.

Make 2.

Make 2.

Make 2.

Make 2.

Make 2.

Figure 3

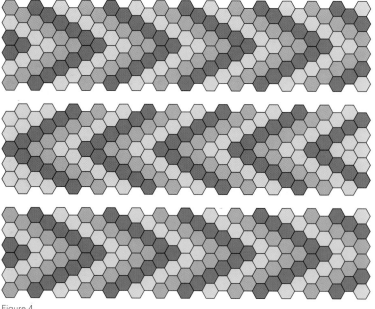

Figure 4

Figure 5

Flying Geese border

1. To create half-square triangles, draw a diagonal line on the wrong side of each 2½″ × 2½″ cream square.

2. Line up 1 square from Step 1 with the edge of a 2½″ × 4½″ rectangle (cut from the fat quarters), right sides together, and the diagonal line on the square running as shown (Figure 6). Sew along the diagonal line, and trim to a ¼″ seam allowance. Open and press.

3. Line up a second square with the other edge of the rectangle, right sides facing, with the diagonal line running as shown (Figure 7). Sew along the diagonal line, and trim to ¼″ seam allowance. Open and press.

4. Repeat Steps 2 and 3 for all 130 rectangles.

Design Note

For a little additional design interest, change the direction of the geese every so often as I did.

5. Arrange and sew the Flying Geese into 2 strips of 31 units and 2 strips of 34 units. Press.

6. Make the corner blocks as shown in Figure 8. Sew 2 cream strips 1½″ × 2½″ to the top and bottom of a brown square 2½″ × 2½″. Press. Sew 2 cream strips 1½″ × 4½″ to the sides of the square. Press. Repeat to make a total of 4 corner blocks.

7. Sew a corner block to each end of the 2 strips of 31 Flying Geese (Figure 9). Press.

8. Sew the 34-piece Flying Geese strips to the top and bottom of the quilt top. Press. Sew the 31-piece strips to both sides. Press.

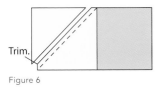

Trim.

Figure 6

Trim.

Figure 7

Figure 8

Finishing

1. Layer and baste the backing, batting, and quilt top.

2. Quilt as desired. I quilted through the center of the hexagons to accentuate the zigzag shape.

3. Use your favorite method to sew the 2½″ binding strips together and bind the quilt.

stars

Star motifs are always a favorite quilt design. Hexagons can be used to make a variety of star shapes such as the spinning stars (*Spinning Wheels*, page 88), six-point stars, and snowflake stars (*Festive Snowflakes Table Runner, page 96*). The best way to get started is to grab a piece of hexagonal graph paper (see Resources, page 159) and sketch the star you want to make. Just keep in mind that star designs can get big quite quickly. For more complicated star shapes, you may need to use 1″ or smaller hexagon templates so the star fits on your quilt top!

Don't be afraid to leave gaps in the stars where the background fabric can peek through, as in the *Giant Star Pillow* (page 82). Less solid shapes make more modern-looking stars. You also can use these gaps for reverse appliqué of motifs.

Giant Star Pillow

Designed and made by Tacha Bruecher

Hexagon sizes: 1″, ¾″ | **Finished size:** 22″ × 22″

Don't be afraid to use prints as a backdrop for your hexagons. Here, I used a subtle print that mimics lined paper, but you could try micro dots, graph-paper prints, basket-weave prints, or other such fabrics. Make sure there is a contrast between the background and the hexagon star. If you choose a bright background, choose light prints for the star, and vice versa.

Traditional hexagon designs can look quite dense. Leaving a few small gaps in the hexagon shapes can give your project a modern feel. Here, the small gaps in the star shape allow the background fabric to peek through and give the star an airy feel.

Materials

Template patterns for the hexagons are on page 157. Copy and cut out 4 paper templates 1″ and 78 paper templates ¾″. See Making Templates, page 18.

- ¾ yard of brown print

- ⅓ yard of plum purple print

- 1 fat eighth of apple green print

- 1 yard of background print

- 1¼ yards of lining fabric

- 26″ × 26″ piece of batting

- 3 strips 2½″ × width of fabric for binding

- 20″ × 20″ pillow form

Design Note

To add more interest to your pillow, use scraps of various plum purple and apple green prints for the hexagons. If you don't have many prints in these colors, perhaps you can arrange to swap with a friend.

Cutting Instructions

From the brown print:

Cut 20 squares 2″ × 2″ for the hexagons on the front and back.

Cut 2 strips 1″ × 16½″.

Cut 2 strips 1″ × 22″.

Cut 4 strips 1″ × 2¾″.

Cut 1 strip 16½″ × 22″ for the back.

From the plum purple print:

Cut 4 strips ¾″ × 16½″.

Cut 2 strips 1″ × 22″ for the back.

Cut 37 squares 2″ × 2″ for the hexagons on the front and back.

From the apple green print:

Cut 21 squares 2″ × 2″ for the hexagons on the front and back.

Cut 4 squares 2½″ × 2½″ for the 4 corners.

From the background fabric:

Cut 1 square 16½″ × 16½″.

Cut 8 strips 1½″ × 16½″.

Cut 4 squares 2¾″ × 2¾″.

Cut 1 strip 8½″ × 22″ for the back.

Cut 1 strip 2½″ × 22″ for the back.

Cut 1 strip 1½″ × 22″ for the back.

From the lining fabric:

Cut 1 square 24″ × 24″ for the front.

Cut 1 rectangle 12½″ × 22″ for the back.

Cut 1 rectangle 16½″ × 22″ for the back.

construction

Refer to Techniques (pages 18–30) for basic hexagon instructions. Press as you go.

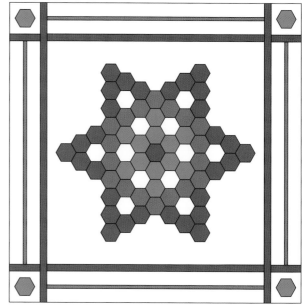

Pillow front layout

Pillow front

1. Sew a background fabric strip 1½″ × 16½″ to each side of a plum purple strip ¾″ × 16½″ along the long edges. Repeat with the other background and plum strips to make 4 matching units (Figure 1).

2. Sew the brown strips 1″ × 16½″ to the top and bottom of the 16½″ × 16½″ background square.

3. Sew 2 of the plum/background units from Step 1 to the top and bottom of the background square (Figure 2).

4. Sew a brown strip 1″ × 2¾″, followed by a background square 2¾″ × 2¾″, to each end of the remaining 2 plum/background units (Figure 3).

5. Sew the brown strips 1″ × 22″, followed by the plum/background units from Step 4, to the sides of the center unit from Step 3 (Figure 4).

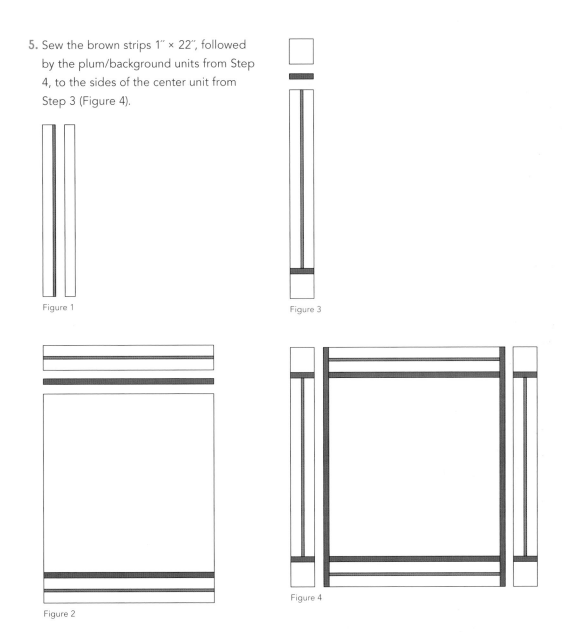

Figure 1

Figure 3

Figure 2

Figure 4

Hexagons

1. Baste the brown, plum, and green 2″ × 2″ squares to the ¾″ hexagon templates.

2. Arrange and sew together 31 plum, 12 green, and 18 brown hexagons into a star shape, leaving the gaps as shown (Figure 5). Press.

> **tip**
>
> Sew the star shape in sections. Start with the center plum/green star, add the brown ring, and finally stitch the plum hexagons in groups of 5 and attach them to the brown ring.

3. Arrange and sew the remaining 17 hexagons in a strip and press. Trim to 22″ long. Set this strip aside to use on the pillow back (Figure 6).

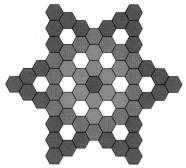

Figure 5

Figure 6

4. Baste the 4 green 2½″ × 2½″ squares to the 1″ hexagon templates.

Quilting

These instructions are for appliquéing and quilting the hexagons by machine at the same time.

1. Layer the pillow front, batting, and 24″ × 24″ square of lining; baste. Position the hexagon star in the center of the pillow front. Pin in place. Remove a pin at a time as you remove all the paper templates, and repin in place. Use a walking foot to stitch the hexagon star in position through all the layers. I stitched inside and outside the center hexagon and stitched the hexagons down around each background gap. Then I stitched all around the outside edges of the star.

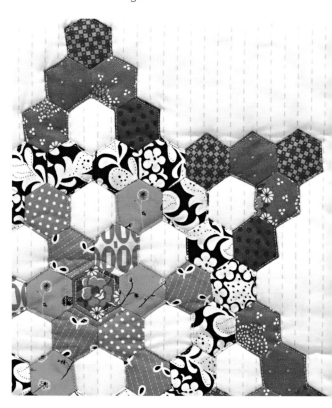

2. Position the corner hexagons in the corner squares and sew in place through all the layers.

3. Add extra quilting as desired.

4. Square up and trim the pillow front to 22″ × 22″.

Pillow back

1. Sew a plum strip 1″ × 22″ to each side of the background strip 2½″ × 22″. Sew the background piece 8½″ × 22″ to the top and the background strip 1½″ × 22″ to the bottom of the plum/background unit. Note that on this pillow back, only 16 hexagons were needed to span the back. Occasionally the shapes "grow" as they are assembled.

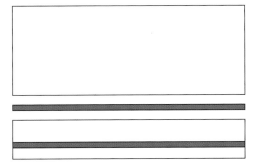

2. Center the 17-hexagon strip on the background 2″ strip. Carefully remove the paper templates and pin in place. Sew around the edges. Trim to a width of 22″.

3. Place the unit from Step 2, right sides facing and raw edges aligned, with the lining piece 12½″ × 22″. Sew along the long outside edge of the background strip nearest the hexagons. Turn right side out, press, and topstitch along the sewn edge.

4. With the brown 16½″ × 22″ and the lining 16½″ × 22″ pieces right sides together and raw edges aligned, sew together along the longest edge. Turn right side out, press, and topstitch along the edge.

Put it all together

1. Lay the pillow front wrong side up, and place the 2 pillow back pieces on top, right sides up. Make sure the previously sewn edges of the pillow back pieces overlap and are lined up with the top and bottom of the pillow front. Pin carefully in place.

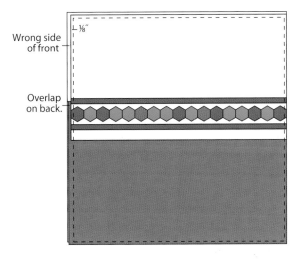

2. Sew all around, ⅛″ in from the edge.

3. Sew together the binding strips, and use your favorite method to bind the edges. Insert the pillow form.

Spinning Wheels Quilt

Designed and made by Tacha Bruecher

Hexagon sizes: 1¾˝, 1˝   Finished size: 62˝ × 45˝

I designed this quilt with my nephew in mind. His head is always spinning with what he wants to build. I thought of him sleeping under this quilt, dreaming of large, mechanical cogs churning around on conveyor belts and making all manner of Lego and Meccano creations!

This quilt is full of color and action. I used a different background fabric for each of the hexagons in the border. It mixes up all the colors used throughout the quilt. Such a busy quilt needs something to help the eye navigate its way around. The solid black softened with black-and-white prints in the Flying Geese strips is perfect for this.

Just imagine what this quilt would look like in linen, pale blue, gray, and a touch of pink! I am itching to make one now. I think this is why I like hexagons so much—they are so versatile.

Materials

Template patterns for the hexagons are on page 157. Copy and cut out 30 paper templates 1¾˝ and 172 paper templates 1˝. See Making Templates, page 18.

- 1½ yards of yellow print A for the block background and vertical strips (½ yard at 42˝ wide if you piece the strips)

- 1 fat quarter of yellow print B for the block background, Flying Geese strips, hexagon borders, and hexagon stars

- 10˝ × 10˝ square each of 3 yellow prints C for the Flying Geese strips, hexagon borders, and hexagon stars

- 1 fat quarter *each* of 8 different red prints for block backgrounds, Flying Geese strips, hexagon borders, and hexagon stars

- 1 fat quarter *each* of 8 different dark blue prints for Flying Geese strips, hexagon borders, and hexagon stars

- 1 fat quarter of black solid fabric for Flying Geese strips

- 1 fat eighth *each* of 3 different black-and-white prints for Flying Geese strips and hexagon borders

- 3⅛ yards of backing fabric

- 70˝ × 53˝ of batting

- 6 strips 2½˝ × width of fabric for binding

Cutting Instructions

From yellow print A:

Cut 1 square 15½″ × 15½″ for the main blocks.

Cut 6 strips 1″ × 45½″ for the vertical strips.*

From yellow print B:

Cut 1 square 15½″ × 15½″ for the main blocks.

From yellow prints B and C:

Cut a *total* of 13 rectangles 2″ × 3½″ for the Flying Geese strips.

Cut a *total* of 4 rectangles 3½″ × 4½″ and 5 squares 4″ × 4″ for the hexagon borders.

Cut a *total* of 5 squares 2½″ for the hexagon stars.

From the red prints:

Cut 6 squares 15½″ × 15½″ for the main blocks.

Cut 2 rectangles 8″ × 15½″ for the main blocks.

Cut 6 lots of 2 squares 2″ × 2″ (cut 2 squares from the same print; then cut 2 squares from a different print; repeat to make 6 lots of 2 squares) for the Flying Geese strips.

Cut a *total* of 13 rectangles 2″ × 3½″ for the Flying Geese strips.

Cut a *total* of 6 rectangles 3½″ × 4½″ for the hexagon borders.

Cut a *total* of 15 squares 4″ × 4″ for the hexagon borders.

Cut a *total* of 5 squares 2½″ × 2½″ for the hexagon stars.

From the dark blue prints:

Cut 4 lots of 2 squares 2″ × 2″ for the Flying Geese strips.

Cut a *total* of 31 rectangles 2″ × 3½″ for the Flying Geese strips.

Cut a *total* of 16 rectangles 3½″ × 4½″ for the hexagon borders.

Cut a *total* of 5 squares 4″ × 4″ for the hexagon borders.

Cut 8 lots of 18 squares 2½″ × 2½″ for the full hexagon stars.

Cut 2 lots of 9 squares 2½″ × 2½″ for the partial hexagon stars.

From the black solid:

Cut 62 squares 2″ × 2″ for the Flying Geese strips.

From the black-and-white prints:

Cut 19 lots of 2 squares 2″ × 2″ for the Flying Geese strips.

Cut a *total* of 3 rectangles 2″ × 3½″ for the Flying Geese strips.

Cut a *total* of 4 rectangles 3½″ × 4½″ for the hexagon borders.

Cut a *total* of 5 squares 4″ × 4″ for the hexagon borders.

If you are piecing the yellow strips, cut 12 strips 1″ × 25″. Sew 2 together as if piecing a binding to get a continuous strip. Trim to 1″ × 45½″. Repeat to make 6 strips.

construction

For basic hexagon instructions, refer to Techniques (pages 18–30).

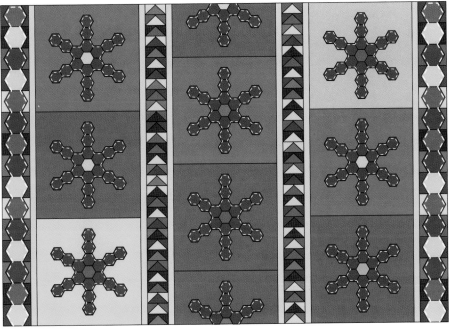

Quilt layout

Main blocks

Piece the 3 main rectangular backgrounds and the narrow yellow strips as shown in Figure 1 (page 92); you will appliqué the hexagon stars (the spinning wheels) later.

1. For the first background column, sew together a yellow and 2 red squares 15½″ × 15½″; press.

2. For the middle background column, sew together a red rectangle 8″ × 15½″, 2 red squares 15½″ × 15½″, and a red rectangle 8″ × 15½″; press.

3. For the third background column, sew together 2 red squares and a yellow square 15½″ × 15½″; then press.

4. Sew the 6 yellow strips 1″ × 45½″ to either side of the 3 background columns as shown in Figure 1; press.

Flying Geese strips

1. Draw a diagonal line on the wrong side from corner to corner on each of the 2″ × 2″ squares (red, dark blue, yellow B and C, and black/white).

2. Pair each rectangle 2″ × 3½″ with 2 matching 2″ × 2″ squares. Line up a square with the edge of its rectangle, right sides together. Sew along the diagonal. Open, press, and trim away the excess seam allowance (Figure 2).

3. Line up the other square with the other edge of the rectangle (Figure 3). Sew along the diagonal; then open. Press and trim away the excess seam allowance.

4. Repeat Steps 2 and 3 for all the rectangles to make 60 Flying Geese units.

5. Arrange and sew the Flying Geese units in 2 columns of 30 Flying Geese units (Figure 4).

Draw diagonal line.

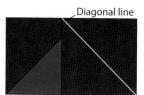

Trim.

Stitch.

Figure 2

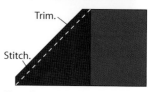

Diagonal line

Figure 3

Figure 1

Figure 4

tip

To make sure the column is straight and the Flying Geese points are not cut off, use a ruler to trim each Flying Geese unit to 2″ × 3½″ before sewing the units into a column. Keep the points intact.

3. Pin the hexagon strips in place on the pieced rectangle borders. Working your way around a hexagon at a time, remove the pin, remove the paper template, and repin in place.

4. Stitch the hexagon strips in place, sewing as close to their edges as possible (Figure 6).

5. Sew together the hexagon border strips with the background blocks/Flying Geese unit. Press.

6. Refer to Figure 5 to sew together the columns of background blocks and the Flying Geese strips. Press.

Hexagon borders

1. Arrange and sew together the red, yellow B and C, dark blue, and black/white rectangles 3½″ × 4½″ in 2 columns of 15 each as shown in Figure 5. Press as you go. Sew these strips to both sides of the quilt top.

2. Baste the red, yellow B and C, dark blue, and black/white squares 4″ × 4″ to the 1¾″ hexagon paper templates. Sew together the hexagons into 2 strips of 15 hexagons each; refer to the colors in the rectangle strips to plan your arrangement.

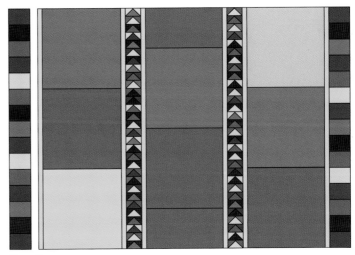

Figure 5

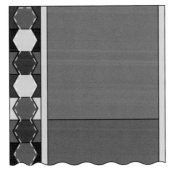

Figure 6

Hexagon stars

1. Baste the red, yellow B and C, and dark blue 2½″ × 2½″ squares to the 1″ hexagon templates to make 172 hexagons.

2. Arrange and sew each group of 18 matching blue hexagons in a star shape. In the center of each star put either a red or a yellow hexagon (Figure 7).

3. Arrange and sew each group of 9 matching blue hexagons in a half-star shape. Use the remaining yellow or red hexagons as the centers (Figure 8).

4. Remove the paper from the center hexagon in each complete star and center each star on a 15″ square. Pin in place. Working your way around each star, a hexagon at a time, remove the pins, remove the paper templates, and repin in place.

5. Stitch the stars in place as close to the edges as possible.

6. Trim the half stars to ¼″ past the middle of the center hexagon (Figure 9). Remove the paper template.

7. Line up the half-star hexagons so that they are centered in the half-square blocks and the raw edge of the cut center hexagon is lined up with the raw edge of the half-square.

8. Pin in place, remove the paper templates and repin as in Step 4, and stitch the half-stars in place.

Finishing

1. Cut the backing to size; layer and baste the backing, batting, and quilt top.

2. Quilt as desired. I used a walking foot to quilt lines ½″ apart vertically down the quilt.

3. Sew the 2½″ binding strips together and use your favorite method to bind the quilt.

Figure 7

Figure 8

Figure 9

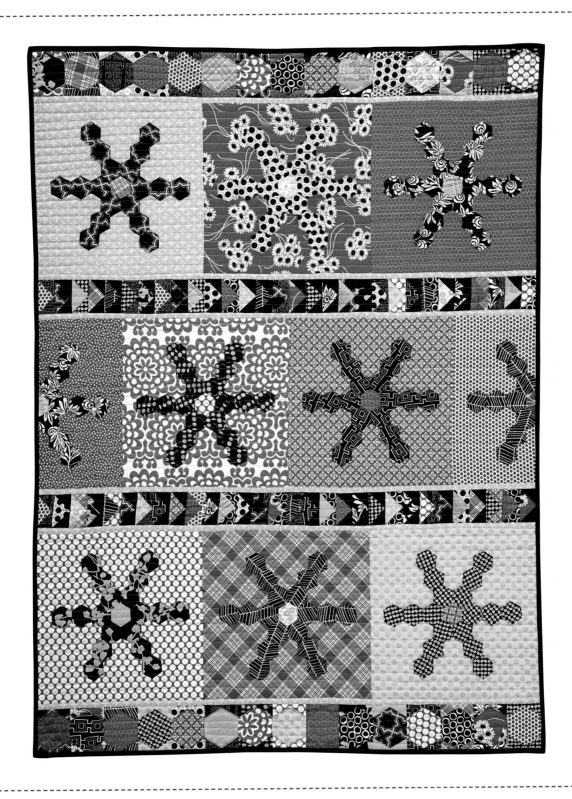

Festive Snowflakes Table Runner

Designed and made by Tacha Bruecher

Hexagon size: ¾″   **Finished size:** 20″ × 56″

With this festive table runner, a few candles, and some Christmas cookies and spiced wine, you are set for jolly holiday fun! The hexagon stars make sprightly snowflakes when you create them from prints. Don't be afraid to use prints that are not specifically for Christmas. Dots, stripes, and damasks in Christmassy colors can give a more timeless feel to your runner. Fussy cut your favorite motifs for the snowflake centers. You could even embroider the centers with a Christmas design.

Materials

The template pattern for the ¾″ hexagon is on page 157. Copy and cut out 126 paper templates. See Making Templates, page 18.

- 8″ × 10″ piece of red background print for snowflakes

- 8″ × 10″ piece of green background print for snowflakes

- 8″ × 10″ piece of white background print for snowflakes

- 1 square 10″ × 10″ *each* of 4 different red Christmassy prints for snowflakes, Flying Geese strips, and triangle border

- 1 square 10″ × 10″ *each* of 4 different green Christmassy prints for snowflakes, Flying Geese strips, and triangle border

- 1 square 10″ × 10″ *each* of 4 different white Christmassy prints for snowflakes, Flying Geese strips, and triangle border

- 3 squares 7½″ × 7½″ of fussy-cut Christmas motifs for snowflake centers

- ⅝ yard of white solid fabric for block background and triangle border

- 15½″ × 15½″ square of light green solid for block background

- 15½″ × 15½″ square of red solid for block background

- ½ yard of dark green solid for Flying Geese strips and borders

- 1¾ yards of backing fabric

- 28″ × 64″ piece of batting

- 5 strips 2½″ × width of fabric for the binding

Cutting Instructions

From the red background print:

Cut 12 squares 2″ × 2″ for the hexagon snowflakes.

From the green background print:

Cut 12 squares 2″ × 2″ for the hexagon snowflakes.

From the white background print:

Cut 12 squares 2″ × 2″ for the hexagon snowflakes.

From the red, green, and white Christmassy prints:

Cut 90 squares 2″ × 2″ for the hexagon snowflakes.

Cut 20 rectangles 3½″ × 2″ for the Flying Geese strips.

Cut 34 squares 3″ × 3″ for the half-square triangle border.

From the white solid fabric:

Cut 1 square 15½″ × 15½″ for the block background.

Cut 34 squares 3″ × 3″ for the half-square triangle border.

From the dark green solid:

Cut 40 squares 2″ × 2″ for the Flying Geese strips.

Cut 4 squares 2½″ × 2½″ for the triangle border corners.

Cut 2 strips 1″ × 15½″ for the inner borders.

Cut 2 strips 1″ × 52½″ (can be pieced) for the inner borders.

construction

For basic hexagon instructions, refer to Techniques (pages 18–30).

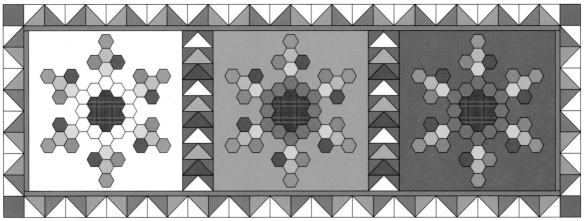

Table runner layout

Hexagon snowflakes

1. Baste the 36 red, green, and white background print 2″ × 2″ squares and the 90 Christmassy print 2″ × 2″ squares to the ¾″ hexagon templates to make 126 hexagons.

2. Arrange and sew the 12 green background print hexagons into a ring (Figure 1). Do the same with the 12 red and 12 white background prints.

3. Arrange and sew the remaining 90 hexagons into 18 groups of 5 (Figure 2).

4. Arrange and sew 6 groups of 5 hexagons from Step 3 and 1 ring from Step 2 into a snowflake shape (Figure 2). Repeat for the other 2 snowflakes.

5. Center each snowflake shape on one of the fussy-cut Christmas print squares. Pin, and hand appliqué each snowflake on top of a print square. Trim the excess fabric away on the back.

6. Center the snowflakes on the 3 red, light green, and white solid fabric background squares 15½″ × 15½″. Pin, and hand appliqué them in place, leaving the hexagon basting and paper templates (Figure 3).

7. Cut away the fabric behind the snowflake to reduce bulk. Remove the hexagon basting thread and the paper templates.

Figure 1

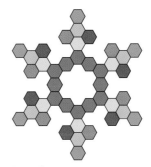
Figure 2

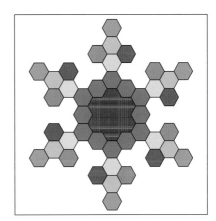
Figure 3

Flying Geese strips

1. Draw a diagonal line from corner to corner on the wrong side of each solid green 2″ × 2″ square.

2. Pair each Christmas print rectangle 3½″ × 2″ with 2 green squares, and line up 1 of the squares with the edge of its rectangle, right sides together. Sew along the diagonal. Open, press, and trim away the excess seam allowance (Figure 4).

3. Line up the other green square with the other edge of the rectangle, right sides together (Figure 5). Sew along the diagonal. Open, press, and trim away the excess seam allowance.

4. Repeat Steps 2 and 3 for all the rectangles to make 20 Flying Geese.

5. Arrange the Flying Geese in 2 strips of 10, and sew together (Figure 6). Press as you go.

> **tip**   Use a white fabric marker on dark fabrics.

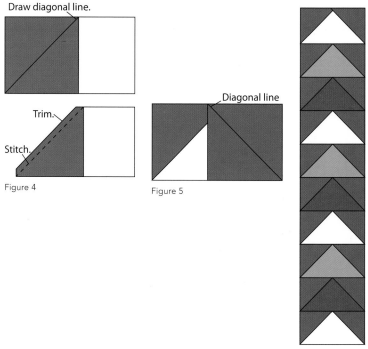

Draw diagonal line.

Trim.

Stitch.

Figure 4

Diagonal line

Figure 5

Figure 6

Half-square triangle border

1. Draw a diagonal line from corner to corner on the wrong side of each white solid 3˝ × 3˝ square. Place a white square and a Christmas print square right sides together, and sew ¼˝ on both sides of the diagonal line. Repeat for all the white and Christmas print squares (Figure 7).

2. For all the units from Step 1, cut along the diagonal line, open, and press. Trim each cut piece to a 2½˝ × 2½˝ square.

> **tip** Line up the seam with the diagonal line on your ruler to make sure the square is even.

3. Arrange the half-square triangles in pairs so that the print triangles form a larger triangle shape (Figure 8). Sew together. Press.

4. Refer to the table runner layout (page 98), and arrange and sew these larger triangles into 2 groups of 13 for the long borders and 2 groups of 4 for the side borders.

5. Sew a 2½˝ dark green square to either end of each group of 4 from Step 4 (Figure 9).

Putting it all together

1. Refer to the table runner layout (page 98) to sew together the table runner blocks, Flying Geese strips, and dark green side inner borders 1˝ × 15½˝. Press as you go.

2. Sew the dark green 1˝ × 52½˝ inner borders to the top and bottom of the runner. Press.

3. Sew the long half-square triangle borders to the top and bottom of the table runner. Press.

4. Sew the short half-square triangle borders to the left and right ends of the runner. Press the seams.

Finishing

1. Layer and baste the backing, batting, and quilt top.

2. Quilt as desired. I quilted straight lines through the Flying Geese strips and echo quilted the half-square triangles on the borders. This runner also would look fabulous with an intricate allover quilting design.

3. Sew the 2½˝ binding strips together and use your favorite method to bind the quilt.

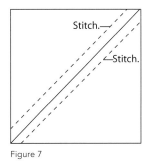

Figure 7

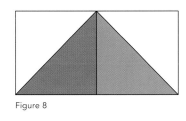

Figure 8

Figure 9

blocks

Rather than sewing hexagons into distinct shapes, you can incorporate panels of sewn-together hexagons into your quilt designs as you would a piece of fabric. Trim the hexagon "fabric" into sections or blocks as shown in the projects in this section. Frame it, cut it into strips, or use it to make half-square triangles. There are so many possibilities. You could even use the sewn-together hexagons as the background fabric for reverse appliqué, in which shapes are cut out of a piece of fabric and the raw edges are turned under to expose the fabric beneath—in this case, the hexagons!

Sunday Brunch Place Mat

Designed and made by Tacha Bruecher

| **Hexagon size:** 1″ | **Finished size:** 18″ × 12¼″ |

Place mats are great for dressing up any table. Make them bold and bright for children or soothing and sophisticated for afternoon tea. You can even match them to your favorite dinnerware!

Use embroidery to make your design pop. Embroider random lines all over your place mat, or stitch motifs such as the knife and fork on these place mats.

I envisioned a relaxing Sunday morning brunch when designing these, so I chose a soothing pink, orange, and gray palette with linen and a splash of embroidery for a modern look.

Materials

The template pattern for the 1″ hexagon is on page 157. Copy and cut out 56 paper templates. See Making Templates, page 18. Makes 1 place mat.

- 56 squares 2½″ × 2½″ of coordinating prints
- 2 rectangles 5½″ × 12¾″ of linen
- 18½″ × 12¾″ piece of backing fabric
- 18½″ × 12¾″ piece of batting
- Embroidery floss and needle
- Chalk or erasable fabric marker

construction

For basic hexagon instructions, refer to Techniques (pages 18–30).

1. Baste the print 2½″ × 2½″ squares to the 1″ hexagon paper templates.

2. Arrange and sew together the hexagons into 7 strips of 8 hexagons. Sew the strips together as shown in Figure 1 (page 106).

3. Remove the hexagon basting and paper templates. Press and trim the block to 8½″ × 12¾″.

4. Sew the 2 linen 5½″ × 12¾″ rectangles to the sides of the hexagon panel from Step 3 (Figure 2, page 106). Press.

5. Put the place mat top and the backing right sides together. Place the batting on top and stitch all the way around, ¼″ in from the edges, leaving a gap in the stitching about 4″ long. Clip the corners and turn the place mat right side out.

6. Press, making sure to fold under the edges at the gap where you turned the place mat. Topstitch around the edge of the placemat (Figure 3), about ¼″ in from the edge. The topstitching should sew the gap closed. You can further secure the gap closed by hand stitching.

Finishing touches

Embroidery patterns are on page 157.

Add an extra touch to your place mats with an embroidered plate, knife, and fork (Figure 4). Use chalk or an erasable fabric marker to draw stitching guidelines.

> **tip** To embroider, make a knot in the end of the thread and, starting about 1″ away from where you want to start your embroidery, take a stitch, bringing the needle out where you want to start the embroidery. Tug on the thread and pull the knot through the top layer, leaving it buried in the batting. Embroider on the guidelines with a running stitch. Stitch through all 3 layers to stop the batting from shifting. Finish by unthreading your needle, making a knot at the last embroidery stitch, rethreading, and tugging it through the top layer.

1. For the dinner plate, draw an 11″-diameter circle in the center of the placemat. Draw a 5¾″-diameter circle inside the large circle. Use a running stitch to embroider both circles.

2. Trace the knife and fork template patterns (page 157) on paper and cut them out. Draw around the templates on your place mat. Use a running stitch to embroider the knife and fork.

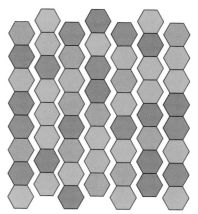
Figure 1

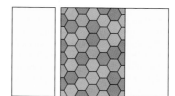
Figure 2

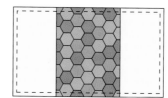
Figure 3

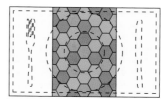
Figure 4

Over the Rainbow Quilt

Designed and made by Tacha Bruecher, and
longarm quilted by Nina Reingruber of http://1001quilt.de

Hexagon size: 1″ | **Finished size:** 112″ × 112″

This is a hex monster! But never fear—help could be near! My quilt top was made with help from my friends in Bee Inspired, a virtual quilting bee made up of quilters from all around the world. For more information on quilting bees, see Quilt with Friends (page 13).

This quilt was created with the help of Bee Inspired members John Adams, Barb Campbell, Ann Christiansen, Donna Weible, Natalie Canadas, Deanna Gipson, Nettie Peterson, Deb Robertson, Lynn Chouw, Meredith McDaris, and Krista Waggoner.

Not only could a bee help lighten the load when it comes to making all these blocks, but you could also organize a swap to get scraps in colors you might not have in your stash. You need only a 2½″ × 2½″ square for each hexagon, and it is fun to have as many different fabrics as possible. (See the Design Note on page 110 for tips on selecting prints.) I am sure many of your quilting friends would be only too happy to do a scrap swap with you. Most of us suffer from overflowing scrap bins!

Materials

The template pattern for the 1″ hexagon is on page 157. Copy and cut out 1,666 paper templates. See Making Templates, page 18.

- 1 fat quarter *each* of 12 different yellow prints*

- 1 fat quarter *each* of 12 different orange prints*

- 1 fat quarter *each* of 12 different red prints*

- 1 fat quarter *each* of 12 different pink prints*

- 1 fat quarter *each* of 12 different purple prints*

- 1 fat quarter *each* of 12 different blue prints*

- 1 fat quarter *each* of 12 different green prints*

- 6 yards of white solid fabric for block framing, sashing, and borders

- 13 strips 2½″ × width of fabric for binding

- 10⅛ yards of backing fabric

- 120″ × 120″ of batting

* Use fat quarters or scraps totaling about 2½ yards of each color.

Cutting Instructions

From the white solid fabric:

Cut 98 strips 1⅛″ × 8¼″ for the block framing.

Cut 98 strips 1⅛″ × 9½″ for the block framing.

Cut 84 strips 2½″ × 12½″ for the sashing.

Cut 2 strips 4½″ × 96½″.

Cut 2 strips 4½″ × 104½″.

Cut 54 squares 4½″ × 4½″ for the outer border.

From each group of prints (yellow, orange, red, pink, purple, blue, green):

Cut 243 squares 2½″ × 2½″ for the hexagons and sashing cornerstones.

Cut 8 squares 4½″ × 4½″ for the outer border.

Cut 14 strips 2½″ × 9½″ for the block framing.

Cut 14 strips 2½″ × 12½″ for the block framing.

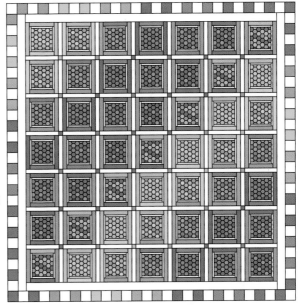

Quilt layout

construction

For basic hexagon instructions, refer to Techniques (pages 18–30).

Hexagon blocks

Block size (unfinished) is 12½″ × 12½″. Make 49 blocks—7 of each color combination (yellow/orange, orange/red, red/pink, pink/purple, purple/blue, blue/green, green/yellow).

1. Set aside 5 each of the yellow, pink, green, orange, red, and purple 2½″ × 2½″ squares and 6 of the blue 2½″ × 2½″ squares for use later as sashing cornerstones. Baste the rest of the 2½″ × 2½″ squares to the 1″ hexagon templates.

2. To make 1 block, choose 17 hexagons of 1 color and 16 of the second color. Arrange and sew them in 3 strips of 5 hexagons and 3 strips of 6 hexagons (Figure 1).

3. Sew the strips together into a block. Remove the hexagon basting threads and templates, press, and trim to 8¼″ × 8¼″ square.

4. Sew 2 white 1⅛″ × 8¼″ strips to the top and bottom of the block. Press. Sew 2 white 1⅛″ × 9½″ strips to the sides (Figure 2). Press.

5. Sew a strip 2″ × 9½″ to the top and another strip 2″ × 9½″ from the same color family to the bottom of the block. Press. Sew a strip 2″ × 12½″ of the second color family to each side (Figure 2). Press.

6. Repeat Steps 2–5 to make 49 blocks.

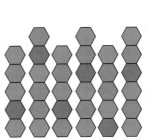

Figure 1

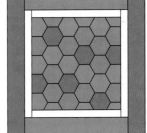

Figure 2

Quilt top assembly

1. Refer to Figure 3 to arrange the blocks in 7 rows of 7 blocks each. Start with a yellow/green block in the upper left corner. Keep the same order of color combinations as shown in each row, but shift each row over by 1 block.

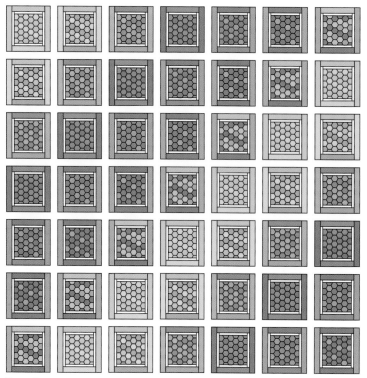

Figure 3

Design Note

When selecting prints, keep in mind that they will be used in blocks of 2 different color combinations. For example, yellow prints will be used in yellow/green blocks and yellow/orange blocks—so choose half that have a green tinge and half that have an orange tinge. Each block needs 33 hexagons, but you will make 34 so you can split the colors as you like. Use the leftovers as a feature on the back of the quilt, in a matching pillow, or in another project.

2. Sew together each row of blocks, placing white sashing strips 2½″ × 12½″ between the blocks (Figure 4). Press.

3. Sew the remaining white strips 2½″ × 12½″ and color print squares 2½″ × 2½″ into 6 horizontal sashing strips as shown in Figure 5. Press.

4. Refer to the quilt layout (page 109) to sew together the rows from Step 2 with the sashing strips from Step 3 between them. Pin well so that the cornerstones match up with the vertical sashing strips properly. Press as you go.

5. Sew the white 4½″ × 96½″ strips to the top and bottom of the quilt top. Press. Sew the white 4½″ × 104½″ strips to the sides. Press well.

6. Sew the white and print 4½″ × 4½″ squares into 4 border strips—2 with 26 squares and 2 with 28 squares—as shown in Figure 6 (page 112). Press as you go.

7. Sew the 26-square border strips to the top and bottom of the quilt top. Press. Sew the 28-square strips to the sides. Press.

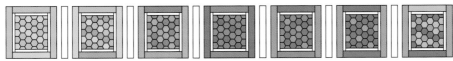

Figure 4

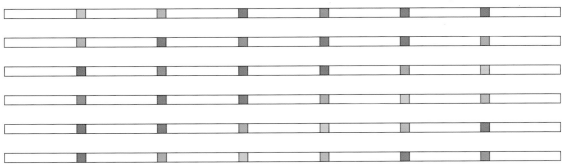

Figure 5

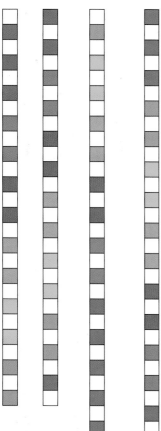

Figure 6

Finishing

1. Cut the backing to size; layer and baste the backing, batting, and quilt top.

2. Quilt as desired. The quilt in the photo was quilted on a longarm machine. Each hexagon block was quilted with a different motif; straight lines quilted through the borders pull the whole thing together.

3. Sew the 2½˝ binding strips together, and use your favorite method to bind the quilt.

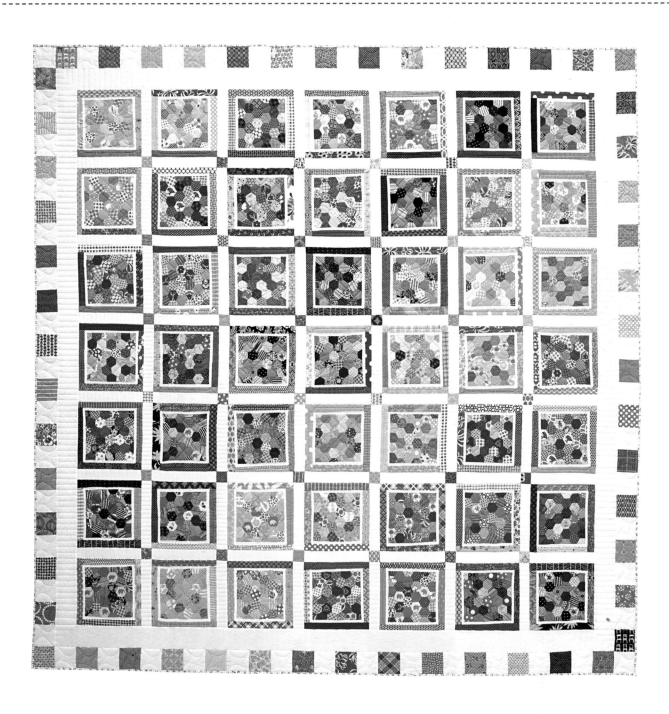

Modern Grandmother's Flower Garden Quilt

Designed and made by Tacha Bruecher

Hexagon size: 1½˝	Finished size: 104˝ × 92˝

One of the best-known hexagon designs is Grandmother's Flower Garden. The classic version features hexagons arranged in rosette flowers and framed by other hexagons made from a solid fabric.

I have modernized the design by isolating the flowers in individual blocks and adding coin strips and sashing strips. Have fun choosing your fabrics, but be careful not to make the quilt too busy. The ring of solid hexagons in each rosette helps focus the eye, as does the dark brown sashing.

This particular quilt was made for a bed with a footboard in mind, so it didn't need the extra overhang at the end. But if your bed doesn't have a footboard, add an extra coin strip and change the layout to 4 blocks × 4 blocks rather than 4 × 3.

This quilt also lends itself well to the quilt-as-you-go technique, so don't be afraid to tackle it on your domestic machine. It is broken down into three sections, each quilted before the sections are joined.

Design Note

Why not get even more modern and set the hexagon blocks in wonky or asymmetrical frames?

Materials

The template pattern for the 1½″ hexagon is on page 157. Copy and cut out 804 paper templates. See Making Templates, page 18.

- ½ yard *each* of dark and medium blue solid fabrics
- ⅝ yard of light blue solid fabric
- ½ yard *each* of dark, medium, and light green solid fabrics
- 8 fat quarters of various green prints
- 8 fat quarters of various brown prints
- 8 fat quarters of various blue prints
- 4 yards of white solid fabric
- 3½ yards of brown solid fabric
- 10⅛ yards of backing fabric*
- 11 strips 2½″ × width of fabric for binding
- 2 pieces 43″ × 112″ of batting
- 1 piece 30″ × 112″ of batting

*Alternatively, you can sew together large scraps to make the backing sections (see Backing and Quilting, page 121).

Cutting Instructions

From the brown solid fabric:

Cut the borders and the vertical sashing strips first, lengthwise.

Cut 4 strips 3″ × 104½″.

Cut 2 strips 4½″ × 104½″.

Cut 15 strips 4½″ × 22½″.

Cut 24 squares 3½″ × 3½″ for the solid hexagon rings.

Cut 4 strips 2″ × 17″ for the block framing.

Cut 4 strips 2″ × 21″ for the block framing.

Cut 4 squares 4½″ × 4½″.

From the dark blue solid fabric:

Cut 12 squares 3½″ × 3½″ for the solid hexagon ring.

Cut 4 strips 2″ × 17″ for the block framing.

Cut 4 strips 2″ × 21″ for the block framing.

From the white solid fabric:

Cut 24 strips 1¼″ × 20″ for the block framing.

Cut 24 strips 1¼″ × 22½″ for the block framing.

Cut 288 squares 3½″ × 3½″ for the hexagons.

From the dark green solid fabric:

Cut 24 squares 3½″ × 3½″ for the solid hexagon rings.

Cut 2 strips 2″ × 17″ for the block framing.

Cut 2 strips 2″ × 21″ for the block framing.

From the medium green solid fabric:

Cut 12 squares 3½″ × 3½″ for the solid hexagon ring.

Cut 4 strips 2″ × 17″ for the block framing.

Cut 4 strips 2″ × 21″ for the block framing.

From the medium blue solid fabric:

Cut 12 squares 3½″ × 3½″ for the solid hexagon ring.

Cut 2 strips 2″ × 17″ for the block framing.

Cut 2 strips 2″ × 21″ for the block framing.

From the light blue solid fabric:

Cut 24 squares 3½″ × 3½″ for the solid hexagon rings.

Cut 4 strips 2″ × 17″ for the block framing.

Cut 4 strips 2″ × 21″ for the block framing.

From the light green solid fabric:

Cut 12 squares 3½″ × 3½″ for the solid hexagon ring.

Cut 4 strips 2″ × 17″ for the block framing.

Cut 4 strips 2″ × 21″ for the block framing.

In total, from the blue, green, and brown prints:

Cut 396 squares 3½″ × 3½″ for the hexagons.

Cut 128 strips 2″ × 4½″ for the coin strips.

construction

For basic hexagon instructions, refer to Techniques (pages 18–30).

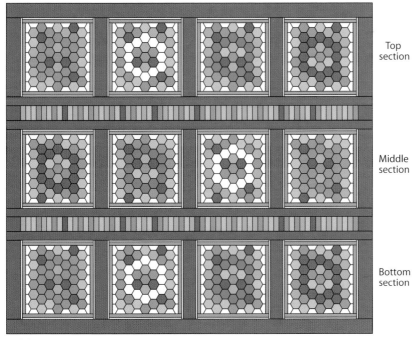

Top section

Middle section

Bottom section

Quilt layout

Hexagon blocks

Block size (unfinished) is 21½″ × 22½″. Make 12 blocks.

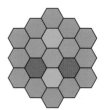

Figure 1

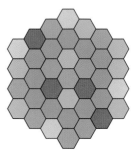

Figure 2

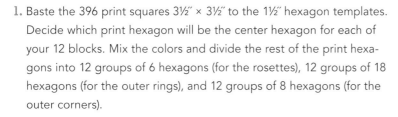

Figure 3

1. Baste the 396 print squares 3½″ × 3½″ to the 1½″ hexagon templates. Decide which print hexagon will be the center hexagon for each of your 12 blocks. Mix the colors and divide the rest of the print hexagons into 12 groups of 6 hexagons (for the rosettes), 12 groups of 18 hexagons (for the outer rings), and 12 groups of 8 hexagons (for the outer corners).

2. Sew a center hexagon and a group of 6 hexagons into a rosette of 7 total hexagons (Figure 1). Repeat to make 12 rosettes.

3. Baste all the green, brown, and blue solid print squares 3½″ × 3½″ and 24 of the white solid squares 3½″ × 3½″ to the 1½″ hexagon templates. Divide these hexagons into 12 groups of 12 matching-color hexagons. Pair each group of 12 solid color hexagons with 1 of the rosettes from Step 2.

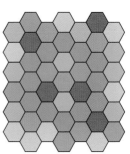

Figure 4

4. Sew a solid ring to a rosette (Figure 2). Repeat to make 12 units. *Note:* As a variation, add different solid colors for the center rings, as I did in my quilt.

5. Sew a ring of 18 print hexagons to each rosette unit from Step 4 (Figure 3).

6. Sew a group of 8 hexagons, placing 2 in each corner, to a unit from Step 5 (Figure 4). Repeat to make 12 units.

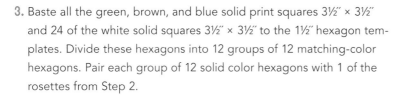
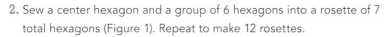

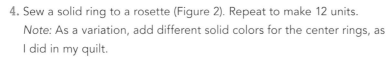

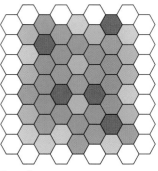

Figure 5

7. Baste the remaining 264 white squares 3½″ × 3½″ to the 1½″ hexagon paper templates.

8. Frame each unit from Step 6 with 22 white hexagons (Figure 5, page 118).

9. Remove the hexagon basting and paper templates. Press and trim each block from Step 8 to 17″ × 18″.

10. Match each block with 2 strips 2″ × 17″ and 2 strips 2″ × 21″ of one of the green, blue, or brown solids. Sew the 2″ × 17″ strips to the top and bottom of a block. Press. Sew the 2″ × 21″ strips to the sides of the block (Figure 6). Press. Repeat for all the blocks.

11. Sew 2 white 1¼″ × 20″ strips to the top and bottom of each block. Press. Sew 2 white 1¼″ × 22½″ strips to the sides of each block (Figure 6). Press well.

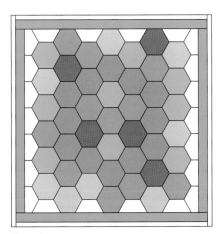

Figure 6

Coin strips

1. Arrange and sew the 128 green, blue, and brown strips 2″ × 4½″ into 2 rows of 64 strips. Press as you go.

2. Sew a brown 4½″ × 4½″ square to the end of each row from Step 1. Press. Sew a brown strip 3″ × 104½″ to the top and bottom of each row (Figure 7). Press.

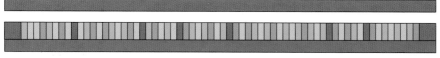

Figure 7

Quilt top sections

Make 3 quilt top sections.

1. Arrange the blocks into 3 rows of 4 blocks each. Sew together each row, sewing the vertical brown strips 4½″ × 22½″ between the blocks and at the beginning and end of each row (see Quilt layout, page 117). Press as you go.

2. Sew the brown strips 4½″ × 104½″ to the top of the top row and to the bottom of the bottom row. Press.

3. Sew the coin row units to the bottom of the top row and to the top of the bottom row. Press.

Backing and quilting

Pieced backing

1. Sew the backing into 3 sections: top section 43″ × 112″, middle section 30″ × 112″, and bottom section 43″ × 112″.

2. Layer and baste each section of the quilt top, batting, and respective backing section.

3. Quilt each section as desired, *but do not quilt* in the top inch of the bottom section, in the bottom inch of the top section, and in the last inch on the top and bottom of the middle section.

Assembly and finishing

1. Fold and pin the backing and batting back from the edges on each section. Take the top and middle sections, and match the long edges of the quilt tops, right sides together; pin. Sew them together through the quilt top only. Press. Repeat for the middle and bottom sections (Figure 8).

2. Trim the batting on each section so that it touches or ever so slightly overlaps the batting in the adjoining section. Whipstitch roughly together.

3. Trim the backing on one section so that it reaches just up to where the quilting ends on the adjoining section. Trim the backing on this adjoining section so that it reaches ½″ past where the quilting ends on the first section (Figure 9). Fold that ½″ of backing fabric under, and press. Pin in place, and hand stitch in place to secure.

4. Repeat Step 3 to join all 3 sections.

5. Fill in with quilting as desired. I quilted straight lines down the seam sections.

6. Use your favorite method to sew the 2½″ binding strips together and bind the quilt.

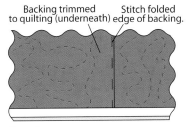

Stitch quilt top sections. Wrong side of backing

Fold batting and backing away from quilt top edge.

Batting

Right side of backing

Figure 8

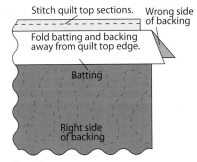

Backing trimmed to quilting (underneath) Stitch folded edge of backing.

Figure 9

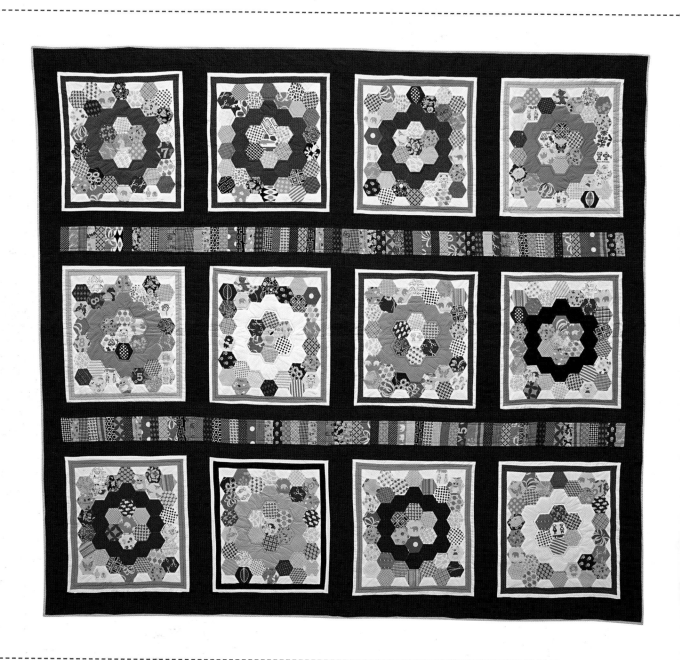

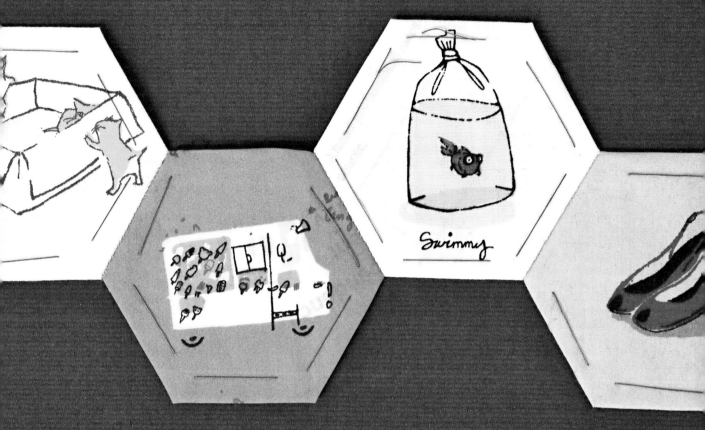

free form

Hexagons don't have to be sewn into specific shapes to be useful design elements; they also can be used in free-form style. Use your hexagons to form any shape or pattern you desire, both abstract and pictorial, like the whimsical appliquéd *Tree House Hideaway* quilt (page 124).

In fact you don't have to sew the hexagons together at all. Single hexagons placed strategically or even scattered around your work can be very effective. Alternatively, bunch a few up in an abstract design on one part of your quilt or spread them out in lines across your whole project. Most of all, just have fun!

Tree House Hideaway Quilt

Designed and made by Tacha Bruecher

Hexagon sizes: ½″, ¾″ | **Finished size:** 25″ × 24½″

Why not use your hexagons to make a picture? Appliqué motifs using the patterns provided, and sprinkle a few hexagons here and there as leaves on a tree. You can even fussy cut motifs such as birds to give your leafy tree added interest.

The tree house in this quilt reminds me of my childhood and making a hideout in the trees at the bottom of the school playing field. We spent hours making it watertight and comfy—all so we could sit in there for about 20 minutes a day and gossip!

Materials

Template patterns for the large tree, the figures, and the hexagons are on pages 157 and 158. Copy and cut out 39 paper templates ½″ and 41 paper templates ¾″. See Making Templates, page 18.

- 1 fat quarter of blue print for background

- 8 squares 8″ × 8″ of different green prints for leaves

- 3″ × 20½″ rectangle of another green print for grass

- ¼ yard of gray print for sashing

- ¼ yard of white solid fabric

- 1 fat quarter of brown print for the tree

- 2 pieces 4½″ × 8″ of brown prints for house and small trees

- 3″ × 3½″ piece of light background print for inside the house

- Scraps for appliqué fabrics for tree house figures

- 17 scraps 1½″ × 2″ of yellow and orange prints

- 1 rectangle 17″ × 6″ of double-sided fusible web

- 28″ × 28″ of backing fabric

- 28″ × 28″ of batting

- 3 strips 2½″ × width of fabric for binding

Cutting Instructions

In total, from the 8″ squares of green prints:

Cut 41 squares 2″ × 2″.

Cut 39 squares 1½″ × 1½″ for the small trees.

From the white solid fabric:

Cut 1 strip 5″ × 25½″.

Cut 3 rectangles 3½″ × 4½″ for the small tree backgrounds.

Cut 6 rectangles 2″ × 3½″ for the small tree backgrounds.

From the gray print:

Cut 2 strips 1½″ × 4½″.

Cut 1 strip 1½″ × 20½″.

Cut 1 strip 1½″ × 25½″.

From the blue print:

Cut 1 rectangle 18″ × 20½″.

In total, from the brown 4½″ × 8″ pieces:

Cut 10 strips 1″ × 1½″ for the tree house.

Cut 1 strip 1½″ × 7″ for the roof.

Cut 1 strip 1½″ × 6″ for the roof.

Cut 1 strip 1½″ × 5″ for the roof.

Cut 1 strip 1½″ × 4″ for the roof.

Cut 3 strips 1½″ × 3½″ for the small tree trunks.

construction

For basic hexagon instructions, refer to Techniques (pages 18–30).

Quilt layout

Main panel

1. To make the background, sew the green strip 3″ × 20½″ to the bottom of the blue rectangle 18″ × 20½″. Press.

2. Enlarge 400% and copy the large tree pattern, and then trace it on the paper side of the fusible web. Cut it out, and iron it to the wrong side of the brown print. Cut it out, remove the paper from the back of the tree shape, and position the tree on the blue/green background (Figure 1, page 128). Follow the manufacturer's instructions to fuse it in place.

3. Machine stitch around the edge of the tree.

4. Use the figures on page 128 to guide you as you make the tree house. Sew the 10 brown strips 1″ × 1½″ into 2 strips of 5. Press. Sew these strips to the sides of the 3″ × 3½″ light background print (Figure 2). Press.

5. Sew together the brown strips 1½″ × 7″, 1½″ × 6″, 1½″ × 5″, and 1½″ × 4″, centering them as shown in Figure 3. Press.

6. Sew this strip set to the top of the house, leaving an overhang of about ¼″. Press and cut into a roof shape (Figure 4).

7. Using leftover scraps from the fusible web, fuse the house shape to the tree branch, referring to the quilt layout (page 126). Stitch in place with black thread.

8. Trace the appliqué shapes for the cat, girl, book, and house roof bunting onto the paper side of the fusible web and cut them out. Fuse them to the wrong sides of your fabric scraps. Remove the paper backings, arrange on the quilt top, and fuse in place. Stitch them in place with black thread.

9. Embroider the faces of the girl and the cat, and use black thread to stitch a rope ladder from the tree house to the ground. I used machine free-motion stitching for the ladder, but you could also embroider the ladder using the backstitch or the chain stitch.

10. To make the leaves, baste the 41 green squares 2″ × 2″ to the ¾″ hexagon templates.

11. Arrange the hexagons in groups on the branches of the large tree. I arranged mine in 2 groups of 2, 1 group of 3, 1 group of 4, 2 groups of 5, 2 groups of 6, and 1 group of 8. When you are happy with the look, stitch the groups together, press, pin in position, and machine appliqué in place.

Figure 1

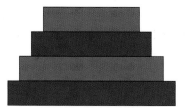

Figure 3

Figure 2

Figure 4

Small trees panel

1. Baste the 39 green squares 1½″ × 1½″ to the ½″ hexagon templates.

2. Arrange and sew the hexagons into 6 rows of 3, 3 rows of 4, and 3 rows of 2. You should have 3 hexagons left over for the tops of the trees.

3. Sew the rows together as shown in Figure 5 to make 3 treetops. Press well. Leave the paper templates in place.

4. Sew the white rectangles 2″ × 3½″ to either side of each of the brown strips 1½″ × 3½″ along the long sides. Press. Sew the white rectangles 3½″ × 4½″ along the top of these strips (Figure 6). Press.

5. Remove the inner templates from the hexagon leaves and pin in place on the white/brown blocks. Hand appliqué the leaves in place (Figure 7).

6. Arrange the 3 tree blocks in a column and sew together, sewing the gray strips 1½″ × 4½″ between them. Press.

7. Sew the gray strip 1½″ × 20½″ to the left of the tree block strip (Figure 8), and sew the panel to the left edge of the main panel. Press.

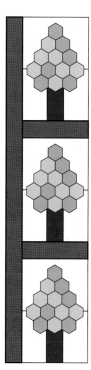

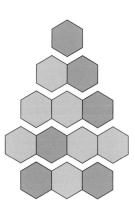

Figure 5

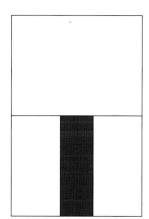

Figure 6

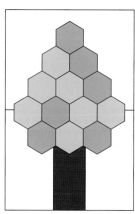

Figure 7

Figure 8

Text border

1. Copy and print the text from the pattern. Make sure you trace the text mirror image onto the paper side of the fusible web. Cut out roughly around each letter, and fuse the letters on the wrong side of the yellow/orange fabric scraps. Cut out the letters.

Design Note

If you want to use a different font or create a different message, the letters should be about 1½″ × 2″.

2. Remove the paper from the back of the letters and arrange them on the 5″ × 25½″ white strip. Using black thread, stitch around each letter to secure it in place.

3. Sew the gray strip 1½″ × 25½″ to the top of the white text strip, and sew this to the bottom of the main panel. Press.

Finishing

1. Layer and baste the backing, batting, and quilt top.

2. Quilt as desired. I hand quilted around the outline of the smaller trees and machine quilted the background of the main picture.

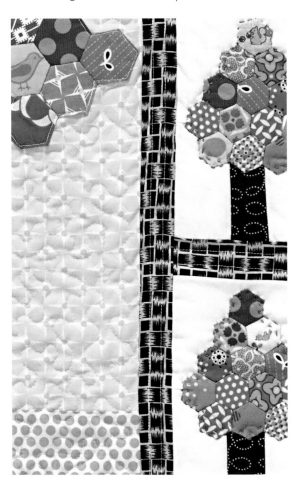

3. Use your favorite method to sew the 2½″ binding strips together and bind the quilt.

Go Faster Box Bag

Designed and made by Tacha Bruecher

Hexagon size: ½″ | **Finished size:** 3″ wide × 4″ high × 8″ long

If you are anything like me, you have a ton of cute Japanese fabric scraps that you just don't know what to do with. You know the ones—Little Red Riding Hood, robots, jumping frogs, and the like. Why not sew them together into zigzag "go faster" strips to adorn a simple box bag? It's just what you need for stashing your hexagons-in-progress—grab and go.

Materials

The template pattern for the ½″ hexagon is on page 157. Copy and cut out 22 paper templates. See Making Templates, page 18.

- 1 fat quarter of lining fabric

- 1 fat quarter of green print fabric

- 14″ × 18″ of stiff fusible interfacing

- 22 squares 1½″ × 1½″ of fabric scraps

- 2 rectangles 2″ × 8½″ of white solid fabric

- 8″ zipper

- 8″ × 9″ piece of dark brown print fabric

- Zipper foot

Cutting Instructions

From the interfacing:
   Cut 2 rectangles 4½″ × 8½″.
   Cut 2 rectangles 3½″ × 4½″.
   Cut 1 rectangle 3½″ × 8½″.

From the green print fabric:
   Cut 4 strips 1½″ × 8½″.
   Cut 2 rectangles 3½″ × 4½″.
   Cut 1 rectangle 3½″ × 8½″.
   Cut 2 strips 1¼″ × 8½″.

From the dark brown print fabric:
   Cut 4 strips ¾″ × 8½″.
   Cut 2 strips 1″ × 8½″.
   Cut 1 rectangle 2″ × 5″.

From the lining fabric:
   Cut 2 rectangles 4½″ × 8½″.
   Cut 2 rectangles 3½″ × 4½″.
   Cut 2 rectangles 2″ × 8½″.
   Cut 1 rectangle 3½″ × 8½″.

construction

For basic hexagon instructions, refer to Techniques (pages 18–30).

Bag front and back

1. Sew a brown strip ¾″ × 8½″ to each side of a white 2″ × 8½″ rectangles. Press. Sew green print strips 1½″ × 8½″ to the brown strips (Figure 1). Press. Repeat to make 2 units: 1 for the front and 1 for the back.

2. Baste the 1½″ squares to the ½″ hexagon templates. Arrange and sew the hexagons in 2 zigzag strips of 11. Press.

3. Center the hexagon strips on the white rectangle front and back pieces. Pin and hand appliqué them in place, removing 1 template at a time. Trim any hexagons that hang over the edge (Figure 2).

4. Iron the 4½″ × 8½″ rectangles of interfacing to the wrong sides of the front and back pieces.

5. Iron the 3½″ × 4½″ rectangles of interfacing to the 3½″ × 4½″ green print fabric rectangles, and the 3½″ × 8½″ rectangle of interfacing to the 3½″ × 8½″ green print fabric rectangle.

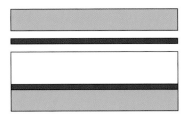

Figure 1

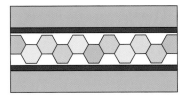

Figure 2

Bag top and loop

1. For the top of the bag, sew the brown strips 1″ × 8½″ to the 1¼″ × 8½″ green print fabric strips. Press.

2. Close the zipper and sew these strips to either side of it, using your zipper foot, with the brown next to the zipper (Figure 3).

3. For the loop, take the brown rectangle 2″ × 5″ and fold under ¼″ on both long sides; press. Fold the strip in half lengthwise with wrong sides together, press, and topstitch 3 lines.

Figure 3

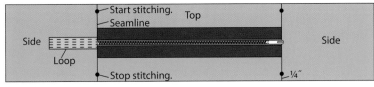

Figure 4

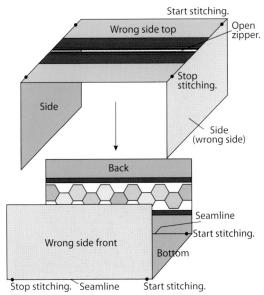

Figure 5

Bag assembly

1. Sew the 3½″ × 8½″ green print fabric rectangle to the bottom edges of the front and back pieces with right sides together. Start and finish the seam ¼″ in from the edges, and backstitch to secure. Press.

2. Pin the 3½″ × 4½″ green print fabric rectangles to the ends of the top zipper strip, right sides facing. Insert the loop in the middle of the seam at the end of the zipper. Stitch, beginning and ending the seams ¼″ in from the edges (Figure 4). Press.

3. Open the zipper and pin the front/bottom/back piece to the side/top/side piece, right sides facing. Stitch, beginning and ending each seam ¼″ from the edge (Figure 5). Press.

4. Clip the corners and turn the bag right side out.

Lining

1. Fold ¼″ under along the long edges on one side of the 2″ × 8½″ lining rectangles, and press.

2. Place the 2 strips of the lining top next to each other so the turned-under edges are just touching; pin the lining top to the short edges of the 3½″ × 4½″ lining rectangles, right sides facing; then sew. Begin and end each seam ¼″ from the edge (Figure 6). This step joins the top and sides of the lining. Press.

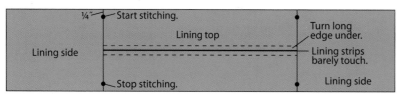

Figure 6

3. Sew the 4½″ × 8½″ lining rectangles to either side of the 3½″ × 8½″ lining rectangle along the long sides. Begin and end each seam ¼″ in from the edge. This step joins the front, bottom, and back of the lining. Press.

4. Pin and sew the top and sides from Step 2 to the front, bottom, and back from Step 3 to make a box shape. Sew all the way around, beginning and ending each seam ¼″ in from the edge. Press.

5. Clip the corners and leave the lining inside out. Insert it into the bag and hand stitch the folded-under edges to the wrong side of the zipper.

6. To keep the lining in place, sew a couple of stitches through the lining, catching a couple of threads of the outer box bag in all the bottom corners.

Stars and Stripes Quilt

Designed and made by Tacha Bruecher

Hexagon size: 1¾″ | **Finished size:** 104″ × 70″

I used to live in North Carolina, and I went to many a 4th-of-July picnic. I would have loved to have whipped out this U.S. flag quilt for our spread! Now that I live in Germany, I plan to use this quilt in our garden for every July 4th—weather permitting, of course…dratted European summers!

This quilt comes together very quickly, although there are a lot of hexagons that make up the stars and stripes. Have fun stenciling your stars with fabric paint, or raid your scrap box and fuse fabric stars to white hexagons.

Materials

Template patterns for the star and 1¾″ hexagon are on pages 157. Copy and cut out 527 paper templates. See Making Templates, page 18.

- ½ yard *each* of 8 aqua prints

- ½ yard *each* of 8 red prints

- 3⅛ yards of red solid fabric

- ½ yard *each* of 8 black-and-white prints

- 4 yards of white solid fabric

- ½ yard of dark blue print for borders (3 yards if you want a continuous piece)

- ½ yard dark blue solid fabric for stars (optional)

- 1 yard double-sided fusible web for stars (optional)

- 112″ × 78″ of batting

- 6½ yards of backing fabric

- 10 strips 2½″ × width of fabric for binding

- Dark blue fabric paint (optional)

- Stencil brush (optional)

- Freezer paper (optional)

Cutting Instructions

From the aqua prints:

Cut a total of 154 squares 4½″ × 4½″.

Cut a total of 26 squares 2½″ × 2½″.

From the red solid:

Cut 3 strips 4½″ × 52½″.

Cut 3 strips 4½″ × 104½″.

From the white solid:

Cut 50 squares 4½″ × 4½″.

Cut 4 strips 4½″ × 52½″.

Cut 3 strips 4½″ × 104½″.

Cut 4 strips 2½″ × 104½″.

Cut 104 squares 2½″ × 2½″.

From the red prints:

Cut a total of 170 squares 4½″ × 4½″.

Cut a total of 26 squares 2½″ × 2½″.

From the black-and-white prints:

Cut a total of 153 squares 4½″ × 4½″.

Cut a total of 104 squares 2½″ × 2½″.

From the dark blue print:

Cut 4 strips 1″ × 104½″.

construction

For basic hexagon instructions, refer to Techniques (pages 18–30).

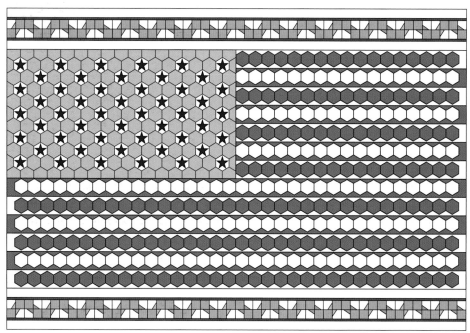

Quilt layout

Star hexagons

1. Baste the 50 white squares 4½″ × 4½″ to the 1¾″ hexagon templates.

2. To make a star stencil, trace the star pattern onto a square of freezer paper and cut it out using a craft knife.

> **tip**
> Use a sharp blade and cut the star shape by pulling the blade toward you into the center of the star shape. Rotate the shape around rather than cutting in different directions. If you make a mistake, repair it with a small piece of tape.

3. Iron the freezer-paper stencil to a white hexagon, making sure to position the star as shown.

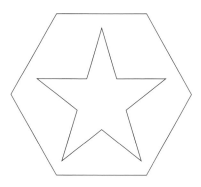

4. Use a stencil brush to dab on the fabric paint; cover the star cutout evenly. Leave it to dry and remove the template. Repeat to make 50.

> **tip**
> Use an up-and-down motion to dab the paint evenly over the template. The same template can be used multiple times, but make sure the paint has dried before ironing the template to another hexagon.

5. Heat set the fabric paint according to the manufacturer's directions.

Design Note

Instead of stenciling stars, you can trace the star pattern onto double-sided fusible web and fuse to dark blue fabric squares cut 3″ × 3″. Cut out and fuse the stars to the center of the white 4½″ × 4½″ squares. Stitch around the edges of the stars to secure them, and then baste the squares to the hexagon templates.

Stars hexagon panel

Baste the aqua, red print, and black/white squares 4½″ × 4½″ to the remaining 1¾″ hexagon templates.

1. Sort the aqua and white star hexagons into 2 groups of 19 aqua hexagons, 5 groups of 6 white star and 12 aqua hexagons, and 4 groups of 5 white star and 14 aqua hexagons.

2. Sew the 2 groups of 19 aqua hexagons into 2 strips.

3. Sew the 5 groups of 12 aqua and 6 white star hexagons into strips as follows:

   1 aqua, 1 white, 2 aqua, 1 white, 2 aqua, 1 white, 2 aqua, 1 white, 2 aqua, 1 white, 2 aqua, 1 white, 1 aqua (Figure 1)

4. Similarly, sew the 4 groups of 14 aqua and 5 white hexagons into strips as follows:

   3 aqua, 1 white, 2 aqua, 1 white, 2 aqua, 1 white, 2 aqua, 1 white, 2 aqua, 1 white, 3 aqua

5. Sew the strips from Steps 2–4 together to make the hexagon star panel (Figure 2). Remove the hexagon basting threads and paper templates. Press and trim to 52½″ × 28½″. Be sure to keep the stars symmetrically placed when you trim. You may lose your first and last columns of aqua hexagons, depending on how much they "grew" during construction.

Figure 1

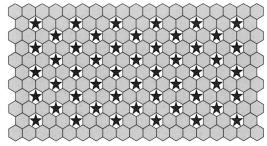

Figure 2

Stripes panels

1. Arrange and sew the red print hexagons into 4 strips of 17 and 3 strips of 34 hexagons. Press.

2. Arrange and sew the black/white hexagons into 3 strips of 17 and 3 strips of 34 hexagons. Press.

3. Sew the flag stripes in 2 sections. Sew the top stripe section together by sewing the red and white strips 4½″ × 52½″ in the following order: white, red, white, red, white, red, white (Figure 3). Press.

4. Center the red hexagon strips on the white strips, and the black/white hexagons on the red strips (Figure 4). Remember to allow for the seam allowances when centering the hexagons on the top and bottom strips! Pin, remove the templates, and repin; machine appliqué in place.

5. Sew the bottom stripe section by sewing the red and white strips 4½″ × 104½″ in the following order: red, white, red, white, red, white (Figure 5). Press.

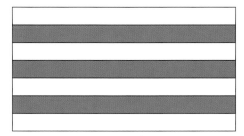

Figure 3

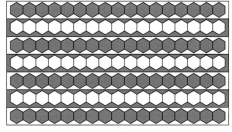

Figure 4

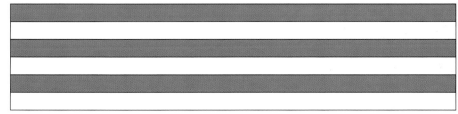

Figure 5

6. Center the red hexagon strips on the white solid strips and the black-and-white hexagons on the red strips, again remembering to allow for seam allowances (Figure 6). Pin, remove the templates, and machine appliqué in place.

7. Sew the top stripe section, the stars panel, and the bottom stripe section together. Don't worry too much about getting the hexagons in each stripe to line up perfectly—close enough is good enough! (See Figure 7.) Press.

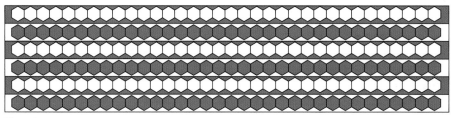

Figure 6

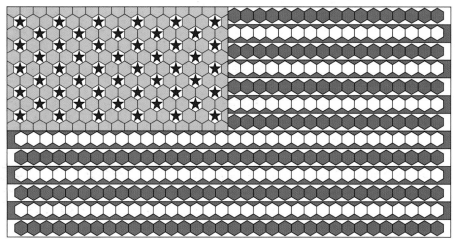

Figure 7

Borders

The borders for this quilt feature unusual wonky triangles.

1. Draw a diagonal line from corner to corner across each of the 26 red and 26 aqua squares 2½″ × 2½″ and cut along the line.

2. Sew each red and aqua triangle to the corner of a white 2½″ × 2½″ square as shown in Figure 8. "Wonkify" your blocks by changing the angle of the triangle.

3. Trim the white square units from Step 2 to 2½″ × 2½″ and remove excess fabric from the seams (Figure 9). Press.

4. Arrange and sew 2 white square units from Step 3 with matching triangles (red or aqua) and 2 matching black-and-white print squares 2½″ × 2½″ into a four-patch (Figure 10). Press as you go. Repeat to make 52 four-patch blocks.

5. Arrange and sew 2 strips of 26 four-patch blocks, alternating the red-and-white and the aqua-and-white blocks (Figure 11). Press.

6. Refer to the quilt layout (page 140) to sew a dark blue strip 1″ × 104½″, followed by a white strip 2½″ × 104½″, to the top and bottom of the four-patch strips from Step 5. Press.

7. Sew the borders to the top and bottom of the quilt top. Press.

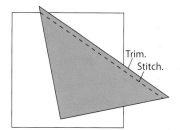

Trim.
Stitch.

Figure 8

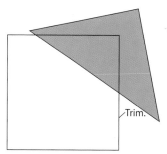

Trim.

Figure 9

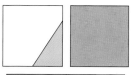

Figure 10

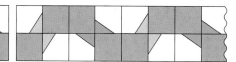

Figure 11

Finishing

1. Layer and baste the backing, batting, and quilt top.

2. Quilt as desired. I stippled the aqua hexagon star panel and quilted straight lines down each of the stripes in the stripes section.

3. Use your favorite method to sew the 2½˝ binding strips together and bind the quilt.

Union Jack Quilt

Designed and made by Tacha Bruecher

Hexagon size: 1¾″ | **Finished size:** 93″ × 64″

You don't have to be a Brit to like the Union Jack design! It is such
a classic and lends itself well to different color palettes. I chose
to use pinks and fuchsias mixed in with red to make a slightly
more feminine version of the flag. Experiment with different color
combinations; consider the look you are going for. It would look
stunning in muted shades of red, white, and blue—or you could
use a completely different palette altogether. I am itching to make
a blue, yellow, and gray version!

I offset the flag design with a funky spiky border. Each spike is
wonkily pieced, in contrast to the exact placement of the hexagons
in the flag design. Make the spikes on your border as wonky and
irregular as you like!

Materials

*The template pattern for the 1¾″ hexagon is on
page 157. Copy and cut out 543 paper templates.
See Making Templates, page 18.*

- ½ yard *each* of 12 different dark
  and medium blue prints

- 1 fat quarter *each* of 14 different
  pink, fuchsia, and red prints*

- 3¼ yards of cream print

- ⅝ yard of off-white print (2⅝ yards
  if you want a continuous border piece)

- 1¾ yards of white solid fabric

- 5¾ yards of backing fabric

- 9 strips 2½″ × width of fabric for binding

- 72″ × 101″ piece of batting

** 11 fat quarters are the minimum required.
I used 14 to expand the color variation.*

Cutting Instructions

In total, from the dark and medium blue prints:

Cut 258 squares 4½˝ × 4½˝ for the hexagons.

Cut about 52 squares 6˝ × 6˝ for the border (see page 154).

From the cream print:

Cut 180 squares 4½˝ × 4½˝ for the hexagons.

Cut 4 squares 5½˝ × 5½˝ for the border corners.

In total, from the pink/fuchsia/red prints:

Cut 105 squares 4½˝ × 4½˝ for the hexagons.

Cut 17 squares 6˝ × 6˝ for the border.

From the off-white print:

Cut 2 strips 2˝ × 80½˝.

Cut 2 strips 2˝ × 54½˝.

From the white solid fabric:

See Borders, page 154, Step 2.

The off-white print in the inner border is used to transition from the cream print in the flag to the white of the border. Choose a print that has small amounts of a complementary color mixed in. I picked an off-white print with specks of green, which complemented both the blue and the pink/fuchsia prints.

Design Note

For the cream print, I chose black text on a cream background. The text is small enough that the cream is still the predominant color, but the text design lends added interest.

construction

For basic hexagon instructions, refer to Techniques (pages 18–30).

Quilt layout

Hexagon Union Jack

1. Baste all the 4½″ × 4½″ squares to the 1¾″ hexagon templates.

2. Divide the blue hexagons into 4 groups of 42, 2 groups of 25, and 2 groups of 20. Vary the prints and their values as you like.

3. Take 1 group of 42 hexagons and sew them into 2 strips of 6, 2 strips of 5, 2 strips of 4, 2 strips of 3, and 2 strips of 2. Leave 2 single hexagons. Sew these strips together vertically into a triangle as shown in Figure 1 (page 152). Repeat for 1 more group of 42 hexagons.

4. Sew the remaining 2 groups of 42 blue hexagons into strips as in Step 3, but this time, sew the strips into a mirror-image triangle (Figure 1).

5. Sew 22 cream hexagons around the outside of each blue 42-hexagon triangle from Steps 3 and 4 (Figure 2).

6. Take 1 group of 25 blue hexagons and sew them into 1 strip of 5, 2 strips of 4, 2 strips of 3, and 2 strips of 2. Leave 2 single hexagons. Sew these strips together vertically to form a triangle (Figure 3).

7. Take the remaining group of 25 blue hexagons and sew them into strips as in Step 6. Sew them into a mirror-image triangle (Figure 3).

8. Sew 24 cream hexagons around the outside of each blue 25-hexagon triangle from Steps 6 and 7 (Figure 4).

9. Take 1 group of 20 blue hexagons and sew them into 2 strips of 4, 2 strips of 3, and 2 strips of 2. Leave 2 single hexagons. Sew these strips together to form a triangle (Figure 5).

10. Take the remaining group of 20 blue hexagons, sew them into strips as in Step 9, and sew into a mirror-image triangle (Figure 5).

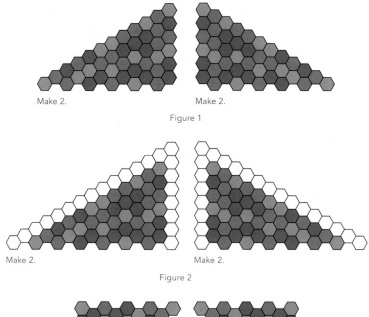

Make 2.　　　　　　　　Make 2.

Figure 1

Make 2.　　　　　　　　Make 2.

Figure 2

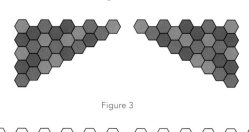

Figure 3

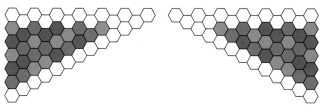

Figure 4

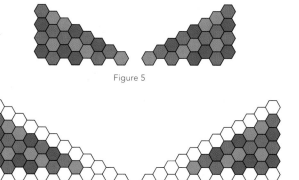

Figure 5

Figure 6

11. Sew 22 cream hexagons around the outside of each blue 20-hexagon triangle from Steps 9 and 10 (Figure 6).

12. Arrange and sew the pink/fuchsia/red hexagons in 4 strips of 15, 1 strip of 17, and 2 zigzag strips of 14 hexagons (Figure 7). The 2 zigzag strips are mirror images of each other.

13. Referring to Figure 8, sew the flag in sections. Start by sewing the 4 corner sections consisting of the blue triangles and pink/fuchsia/red strips of 15 hexagons together to form 4 rectangles. Sew these rectangles to either side of the horizontal red zigzag strips, and then sew these sections to either side of the middle pink/fuchsia/red strip of 17 hexagons.

14. Press, remove the hexagon basting threads and templates, and trim to 80½″ × 51½″.

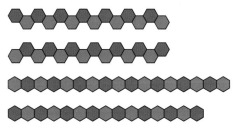

Figure 7

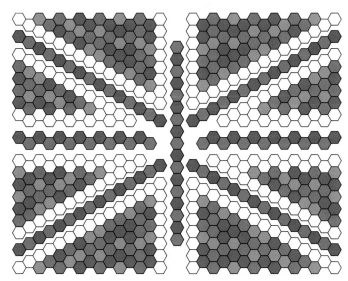

Figure 8

Borders

1. Sew the off-white strips 2″ × 80½″ to the top and the bottom of the Union Jack. Press. Sew the off-white strips 2″ × 54½″ to the sides. Press.

2. Cut the white solid fabric into strips 5½″ × width of fabric. Cut each of these strips into pieces ranging in size from 2½″ × 5½″ to 4½″ × 5½″ (Figure 9). The number of pieces you need will depend on how wide each 5½″ piece is. Don't worry about cutting all the pieces at once. Start with 80 and begin making the border strips. Cut more pieces as you need them.

3. Cut the blue and the pink/fuchsia/red 6″ × 6″ squares in half diagonally. Take each triangle and sew it to a white piece. Press. Make sure that when the triangle is opened up and pressed, it covers the corner of the white piece (Figure 10).

4. Turn the white piece over and, using the edges of the white piece as a guide, trim it to its original size (Figure 11). Trim the excess from the seam allowance.

5. Sew together the white triangle pieces, making sure the triangles all point to the same side. Keep sewing pieces together until you have 2 strips 5½″ × 83½″ and 2 strips 5½″ × 54½″. Press.

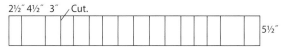

2½″ 4½″ 3″   Cut.

5½″

Figure 9

Figure 10

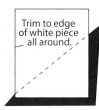

Trim to edge of white piece all around.

Figure 11

Design Note

Play with the wonkiness of the border by sewing the triangles at different angles and mixing up the width of the white pieces. Keep the border width consistent at 5½″ including the seam allowances.

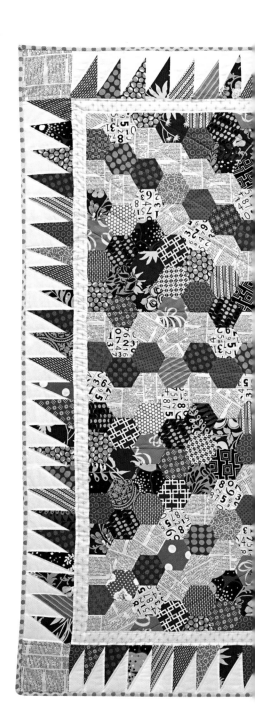